MAGIC CELTIC GODS and GODDESSES

A Guide to Their Spiritual Power, Healing Energies, and Mystical Joy

MAGIC OF THE CELTIC GODS and GODDESSES

A Guide to Their Spiritual Power, Healing Energies, and Mystical Joy

Carl McColman and Kathryn Hinds

NEW PAGE BOOKS
A division of The Career Press, Inc.
Franklin Lakes, NJ

MAGIC OF THE CELTIC GODS AND GODDESSES
EDITED BY GINA M. CHESELKA
TYPESET BY STACEY A. FARKAS
Cover illustration and design by Jean William Naumann
Printed in the U.S.A. by Book-mart Press

To order this title, please call toll-free 1-800-CAREER-1 (NJ and Canada: 201-848-0310) to order using VISA or MasterCard, or for further information on books from Career Press.

The Career Press, Inc., 3 Tice Road, PO Box 687,
Franklin Lakes, NJ 07417
www.careerpress.com
www.newpagebooks.com

Library of Congress Cataloging-in-Publication Data

McColman, Carl.
    Magic of the Celtic gods and goddesses : a guide to their spiritual power, healing energies, and mystical joy / by Carl McColman and Kathryn Hinds.
        p. cm.
    Includes bibliographical references and index.
    ISBN 1-56414-783-5
    1. Magic, Celtic. 2. Gods, Celtic—Miscellanea. I. Hinds, Kathryn, 1962- II. Title.

BF1622.C45M335 2005
299'.16--dc22   2004058461

Dedication

To Christina, for showing me this path

–k.h.

To Gwen, for walking the path with me

–C.M.

Acknowledgments

First and foremost, we would like to thank our spouses, Fran McColman and Arthur Hinds, for their invaluable support and input on this project. We must also thank our students for keeping us continually on our toes—because of them, our own learning process never stops. Many kudos to our agent, Linda Roghaar, and to Mike Lewis, Gina Cheselka, and all the other good people at New Page for their faith in this book and their hard work in getting it to print. And finally, our gratitude to Brice and the staff of the Coffee Shop of Horrors in Gainesville, Georgia, for not only putting up with us during our lengthy brainstorming sessions, but for keeping us comfortable and well-caffeinated the whole time.

Contents

Part One: Introduction

Part Two: Goddesses and Heroines

Part Three: Gods and Heroes

Part Four: Goddesses and Gods in Our Lives

Part One:

Introduction

Chapter 1

Entering the Otherworld

 e'd like to invite you into a fascinating world.

It's a world shaped by history and mythology, by ancient stories and modern spiritual yearning. It's a mystical world where mortals encounter immortals, where humans live and love alongside powerful beings who can only be called gods and goddesses. It's a world of magic and miracles, of heroes and heroines with extraordinary abilities who fight fearsome enemies and heart-stopping demons. It's a world where virtues such as honor, hospitality, courage, wisdom, and sovereignty (freedom) matter—where both gods and mortals are willing to fight and die for such eternal values.

Finding your way into this world today is a challenge, for only fragments of stories and legends and lore about this magical realm have come down to us from our ancestors of old. And yet, enough information exists that we can piece together a picture of this majestic world and make it our spiritual home. Indeed, both of us (Carl and Kathryn) have found our mystical center in this world and, through our visionary excursions there, embraced a spirituality of meaning, power, love, and joy. And now we invite you to journey there with us.

This world is the realm of Celtic myth. It is a place of promise, of eternal youth, of frightening conflict, but of glorious victory. It is a place brimming with mythic beings, some of whom are truly deities; others are semi-divine; others are gifted, but mortal, heroes and heroines. (For simplicity's sake, we'll refer in this book to the entire community of mythical beings as gods and goddesses.)

Alas, the Celtic mythological realm—often called the "Otherworld"—is also a place deeply shrouded in mystery and frequently misunderstood. We have no bible or sacred text to tell us everything we need to know about this world—instead, to find our spiritual home, we must rely on a variety of sources, from archaeology to medieval manuscripts to living folklore, none of which give us a comprehensive picture of ancient Celtic spirituality, but all of which, taken together, provide a tantalizing overview of the beauty and glory that our ancestors found in their dealings with their gods and goddesses.

Incidentally, when we talk about our ancestors, they can be understood in two ways. If you come from a Celtic land, such as Wales, Ireland, or Brittany, then you can claim the Celts as your biological ancestors. But even if you don't have a single strand of Celtic DNA, you could still claim the Celts as your *spiritual* ancestors—ancestors of the heart. Either way, the magical realm of Celtic myth comes to us from our ancestors—and it is our great privilege here in the 21st century to call out to the gods and goddesses of our ancestors, to honor and venerate them, and to breathe new life into this ancient and noble spiritual path.

This book is by no means an exhaustive introduction to the spirituality of Celtic myth. Far from it! Rather, it is kind of like a first date. When you go out with someone for the first time, your evening is spent getting to know each other just enough to decide if it would be nice to keep dating. Similarly, our hope for this book is to give you enough of an introduction to some of the major gods and goddesses of the Celtic world so that you can decide if Celtic spirituality is something you'd like to pursue seriously (if so, you'll find many books that can help you deepen your relationship with the gods and goddesses listed in Appendix A and the bibliography).

An Often Misunderstood Spirituality

The realm of Celtic myth is often misunderstood among today's spiritual seekers. Many people feel drawn to the magic of the Celts, whether because of their ancestry, their spiritual inclinations, or simply their love for a romantic ideal that is epitomized in fairy stories and legends of Merlin and King Arthur. Sadly, though, relatively little reliable literature seems to be available on what the ancient Celts truly believed, and about the many gods and goddesses they worshipped (scholars have identified well over 400 Celtic gods and goddesses!). Most of the books being published are either fascinating (but expensive and hard to find) scholarly and academic monographs, or else New Age titles that are written for a wide readership, but too often seem to lack any real grounding in the exciting world of Celtic spirituality as it truly existed (and has been documented in medieval manuscripts as well as in modern Celtic folklore). In fact, we recommend that whenever you read a book that claims to offer spiritual teachings from the Celtic world, check the bibliography: Did the author take the time to do research into the history of the Celts, or is the teaching mostly based on the author's own psychic or intuitive ideas? Even if the author has good intentions, we would encourage you to stick with books that are grounded in solid research because so much of the material that has been published about the Celts has, alas, been based in subjective fantasy rather than reliable history.

In *Magic of the Celtic Gods and Goddesses*, we are attempting to bring the two worlds of scholarship and spirituality together. With this book, we are not contributing anything new to the academic world of Celtic studies, but rather we are drawing on what Celtic scholars have discovered about the ancient lore, and presenting this knowledge in a way that can be applied to modern spirituality. Of course, this is a project fraught with danger—for even with all the archaeological research and studies of medieval manuscripts and Celtic folklore that have been conducted over the years, there are still far too many holes in our knowledge. Anyone who wishes to honor the old gods and goddesses in a meaningful way today will have to adapt what little we know to the demands of modern life—and fill in the many gaps, as best we can, with our 21st century sensibilities, hoping to steer our spirituality in a direction that is both meaningful for us and pleasing to the deities.

Why Bother?

Before we go any further, let's consider for a moment why anyone should bother studying, let alone honoring or venerating, the old gods and goddesses of the Celtic tradition. What is the point of bringing these deities "back to life" in today's world?

We believe there are many benefits to a renewed Celtic spirituality. Here are just a few thoughts on this matter. As you explore your unique relationship with the gods, you may find your own reasons for pursuing a spiritual connection with them.

The gods and goddesses connect us with the Celtic soul. This is really just a restatement of the first part of this chapter. The deities and mythic heroes of Ireland, Wales, and Gaul do not exist in a vacuum; they arise out of a culture of magic, poetry, storytelling, and valor. Their spirit is, truly, the Celtic spirit. If we want to walk the Celtic path, it begins by getting to know these powerful entities. And the best way to get to know them is through entering their natural "habitat"—the realm of stories, myths, legends, and lore.

The deities connect us with our ancestors. As we've said, whether we regard the ancient Celts as biological forebears or simply ancestors of the heart, they have played a decisive role in shaping who we are today. Celtic spirituality, like most other primal faiths, emphasizes the importance of honoring the ancestors. What better way to do that than by getting to know (and venerating) their gods and goddesses?

The deities connect us with a Celtic understanding of the cosmos. Spirituality is more than just a psychological tool for achieving happiness or feeling at peace with the world—it is a tool for knowing who we are and where we fit into the universe. Celtic spirituality, therefore, invites us to relate to the cosmos from a specifically Celtic perspective. This includes seeing the universe as filled with the presence of ancestral and divine spirits, regarding nature herself as sacred, and seeing such things as rivers, wells, stones, trees, mountains, fire, and countless other elements of the cosmos as filled with luminous meaning—in short, with soul. It means seeing death not as the end of life, but as a transition to a visionary world known as the Land of Promise or the Land of Youth (among other appellations). It means believing that the spiritual Otherworld is interwoven with the physical world in such a way that assumes the nearness, rather than the remoteness, of divinity in the cosmos. All this, and more, is to be found through the Celtic gods and goddesses!

Their stories can help us find meaning in our lives. Like many mythic tales from cultures around the world, the stories of the Celtic deities and heroes cover a wide emotional and dramatic terrain. In these stories we encounter passionate love, treacherous duplicity, fearless courage, raw sex, clever trickery, honest effort, trusting patience, hopeful perseverance, and countless other feelings and actions. Through the richly textured lives of the mythic heroes, we find ways to understand the emotions and passions of our own journeys. Not only that, but these stories are often entertaining, suspenseful, and at times really humorous. All of these elements in the myths, of course, are aspects of the spiritual world that find reflection in our mundane universe.

The deities can be a gateway to believing and living in an alternative way. A wise Irish priest once told me (Carl) that Celtic spirituality is about having an "alternative vision"—in other words, being able to see things in ways other than what big government, big business, or big religion would have us see. Celtic spirituality is a path of hope through choices, and the mythic lives of the gods and goddesses can help us recognize those choices and alternative visions. For example, the Celtic myths invite us to see the cosmos in terms of polytheism (many gods and goddesses) rather than the strict monotheism of most major religions. The gods and goddesses are healers and warriors striving to make their world a better place, not just giving into forces that may appear to be bigger than they are. Most of all, through the deities and heroes and their dramatic tales, we can remember that Celtic spirituality stands for eternal values; for a world where consumerism and materialism are not the dominant powers that shape our lives. Celtic spirituality gives us hope that there's more to life than what can be found at the mall.

The deities personify the reality of magic beyond the physical universe. Magic and *mysticism* are loaded words subject to misinterpretation and all sorts of confusion. For now, let's just say that magic (the exercise of spiritual power) and mysticism (the journey toward spiritual bliss and enlightenment) invite us to a deeper or higher experience of life than we can normally encounter in the mundane physical world we inhabit. This is another aspect of the alternative vision of Celtic spirituality—but here, the gods and goddesses invite us to make that alternative vision part of our own personal experience so that we can transform the universe—from the inside out. When we learn the ancient lore or encounter the deities through ritual or meditation, we are invited to become students of their spiritual power and conduits for their luminous joy.

The gods and goddesses are a source of blessing and power. If there's one reason why anyone, of any religious persuasion, pursues the spiritual life, it's probably this: to receive blessings. It's a universal part of spirituality— from the Catholic Mass, which always ends with the priest blessing his congregation, to modern druid ceremonies such as those practiced by Ár nDraíocht Féin (America's largest druid organization)—built around the universal human desire to receive spiritual benefits in their lives. A key incentive to prayer and magic is the quest for blessings of some sort—to manifest desires that are quite earthly in nature (a new job, a new girlfriend), or more "spiritual" yearnings (peace of mind, a sense of purpose). Connecting with the Celtic deities means opening up a channel to ask for, and receive, blessings from them.

The deities help us to become better people. Blessings are wonderful, but they are only half of the value of spirituality. Equally important for any spiritual or religious path is the way it supports its adherents in finding healing, maturity, virtue, and holiness. Celtic spirituality is holistic, so it's not just about becoming a paragon of self-denial (in fact, in the Celtic world that would not necessarily be seen as a good thing). Rather, it supports us in becoming well rounded and whole: It advocates courage and physical strength, wisdom and mental ability, magic and spiritual prowess, but also old-fashioned virtues such as honor (treating others with respect), hospitality (sharing of your abundance with others), and integrity (being a person of your word). How do the gods facilitate this? They model the virtues that are worth cultivating—as well as sometimes exhibiting the foibles of a life without virtue or self-improvement!

The deities remind us of our own divinity. There are many different ways to approach the gods and goddesses of Celtic (or any) mythology. In Chapter 3, we'll look at possible ways to think about the deities, but it is not the purpose of this book to tell you what to believe. That being said, we would like to end this chapter by making a case for deity or godhood being something that flows with abundance from the Otherworld to our mundane world. Not only are the gods and goddesses divine, but also the fairies (the spirits of the natural world), and the ancestors partake in their divinity. As Celtic lore sees it, our universe shimmers with sacred presence—and you and I share in this divine plenitude. The gods are not "way up there" and we mortals "way down here." On the contrary, the gods live in our minds and hearts. We are their sacred temples; our bodies are the altars where they are worshipped and adored. The Celtic gods and goddesses invite us to experience our own divinity and, by doing so, to join them in the ever unfolding task of creating and re-creating the cosmos in which we live. New Agers love to say, "You create your own reality." In the Celtic cosmos, it's seen a bit differently: We mortals join with the deities in co-creating all things.

Many benefits and blessings can flow from a spirituality centered on the Celtic heroes and deities. We hope that as you learn about the different gods and goddesses and explore ways to honor them in your own life, you will discover for yourself how they are bringers of joy and blessing. May your journey into their divine presence be delightful and fruitful—and may the information in this book help you to find your own way into the magical Celtic Otherworld.

Chapter 2

An Overview of the Celtic Tradition

The Celtic spiritual tradition is a multifaceted jewel. Some of these facets are Christian; the ones we discuss in this book are Pagan. This means that we are working with pre-Christian notions of the divine and its relationship to human life. These ideas have been treated in a variety of ways throughout the past 15 or so centuries: They've been rejected, reinterpreted, rediscovered, reconstructed; studied, sometimes romanticized, often misunderstood. The bottom line is that in spite of (and sometimes because of) all that the worship of the old goddesses and gods has been through, it has survived, and continues to live and grow.

The Celtic Pagan traditions that we now work with cannot help differing from those of the distant past. We have lost so much ancient lore; we have so little knowledge of ancient religious practices—and the lore, beliefs, and practices that have survived to the present have come to us garbed in extra layers accumulated through the centuries. Time, language, technology, the ways that Western culture has developed—these and other factors have placed us at a great distance from the ancient Celts. For a large number of us, that distance is compounded by geography: We live an ocean away from the continent and the islands where Celtic spirituality developed, flourished, and, to a greater or lesser extent, remains embedded to this day. Our first step toward a fuller understanding of Celtic deities, then, is to go back to their roots.

At this point, we need to answer a fundamental question: What do we mean by *Celtic*? Well, there is actually a fair amount of debate among scholars over this term. Some prefer to use it in a narrow sense, restricting it to the Celtic branch of the Indo-European language family. The modern Celtic languages are Irish, Manx, Scottish Gaelic, Welsh, Breton, and Cornish. In ancient times, Celtic dialects were spoken from Ireland to Romania, as well as in the central Turkish region of Galatia. Gaulish, the Celtic tongue of what is now France and Belgium (with parts of Germany, Switzerland, and the Netherlands) was in everyday use until about the fifth century, and is the most ancient Celtic language in which we have any written records, in the form of inscriptions on altars and the like.

A number of scholars give *Celtic* not only a linguistic but also a cultural meaning: The Celts were a group of peoples who shared a common language (with many dialects or variants) and a common culture—similar ways of making and decorating material goods, similar ways of organizing society, similar ways of approaching religion. On top of this, *Celtic* can also refer to an ethnic group—people who share not only language and culture, but also a common place of origin. In this book, we use *Celtic* in the combined linguistic and cultural sense, and leave the question of ethnicity for scholars to debate.

Sources for the Tradition

Throughout this book, we will refer to three principal sources for Celtic Pagan spiritual traditions: archaeology, literature, and folklore. Archaeology provides us with information through images, inscriptions, burials, building sites, and other material remains of Celtic culture. Archaeological evidence can, however, be difficult to interpret—often we can only guess at what religious use or meaning (if any) an object may have had or at how the ancient Celts meant various symbols in their artwork to be interpreted. Nevertheless, the material unearthed and studied by archaeologists is invaluable to us.

The earliest literary evidence for Celtic religion (and other aspects of Celtic culture) was written by various Greek and Roman authors. Not all of this material is entirely reliable. Few classical authors attempted to make full and objective studies of Celtic peoples; most of these writers employed descriptions of the Celts in service of their own aims, whether it was Caesar justifying his conquest of Gaul or Tacitus using the idea of the "noble savage" to criticize Roman decadence. If we read these authors critically, however, we can nevertheless glean a great many useful insights.

Celtic peoples did not start writing their own literature until the early Middle Ages, after the adoption of Christianity established the written word as the primary means for preserving and transmitting knowledge. Irish and Welsh were the languages used for recording most of the surviving mythological material. Irish, of course, was and is the language of Ireland (Éire). Welsh (or Cymraeg), however, was initially not limited to Wales (Cymru), but was spoken and used through most of the island of Britain—Prydain, the Isle of the Mighty. In fact, the earliest surviving poem written in the Welsh language (*The Gododdin*) comes from what is now the English-Scottish border region. Eventually, English became the dominant language in most of southern Britain, but it is important to remember that stories recorded in the Welsh language may reflect the mythological traditions of other parts of Britain as well as of Wales.

Scholars today typically organize the main Irish tales into four groups: the Mythological Cycle (tales of goddesses and gods), the Ulster Cycle (tales of King Conchobar mac Nessa and the warriors surrounding him, especially Cú Chulainn), the Fenian Cycle (tales of the warrior-poet Fionn macCumhail and his associates), and the Historical Cycle or Cycle of the Kings. There is ample evidence, however, that the Irish poets and storytellers themselves organized their lore thematically: Wooings, Elopements, Births, Boyhood Deeds, Battles, Cattle Raids, Journeys, and so on. This thematic trend also shows up in Welsh literature, most famously in the Triads of the Island of Britain (the "Welsh Triads"), which catalog a vast lore into groups of three; for example, "Three Enchanters of the Island of Britain: Coll son of Collfrewy, and Menw son of Teirgwaedd, and Drych son of Kibddar" (Triad 27). The Triads, alas, for the most part only hint at stories, most of which are lost to us. The primary sources we have for British or Welsh mythology are the stories known as the Four Branches of the Mabinogi, plus a small number of other mythological tales.

Additional literary evidence for Irish goddesses and gods comes from the legendary history *Lebor Gabála Érenn*, "The Book of the Taking of Ireland" (or "Book of Invasions"), and from several medieval "catalog"-type works, such as the Dindsenchas, a collection of lore connected with the landscape. Early Irish and Welsh literature alike also contain a handful or two of miscellaneous poems, genealogies, and other records that shed further light on Celtic deities.

Where literature leaves off, folklore takes over. Authors of the 16th century attested that tales of the ancient deities and heroes were still being told in Wales and the Scottish Highlands; two centuries later, folklorists began in earnest to record these stories, along with various folk beliefs and practices of Ireland, Scotland, Wales, and Cornwall. Numerous traditional tales and practices survived through to the 20th century, and in many of them we can see echoes, hints, or continuations of aspects of ancient Celtic religion. Today, unfortunately, the living oral tradition appears to be dying out in the face of mass media that reaches even the remotest villages. This makes the material collected by generations of folklorists, from storytellers and other tradition bearers, especially precious.

Some General Principles of Celtic Mythology

As we've mentioned earlier, scholars have identified hundreds of Celtic deity names. Of more than 400 goddess or god names found in inscriptions, 300 appear only once. This is because much of Celtic religion was intensely local—deities were identified with very specific places, such as a spring or hill or a grove of trees. For the Celts, nature was enspirited with divine forces, and, in a great many cases, a goddess or god was first and foremost the "spirit of the place." Even in medieval Celtic literary texts, this intimate link with place remains strong—in the Fourth Branch of the Mabinogi, for example, the stories of the gods Lleu and Gwydion are full of references to very specific locations in north Wales where the tales' events occurred.

Another reason for the plethora of deity names is that they are often really titles and not, strictly speaking, personal names. Among the titles we find are "The Exalted One" (Irish Brigit, northern British Brigantia), "The Bright One" or "Shining One" (Welsh Lleu, Irish Lugh, Gaulish Belenus), "The Son" (Welsh Mabon), "The Good Striker" (Gaulish Sucellus), "The Great Provider" (Gaulish and British Rosmerta)—you get the idea. It is possible that, at least in some cases, different local titles may in fact refer to basically the same deity.

On the other hand, in the literature we find deities whose names are Irish and Welsh versions of one another—such as Irish Goibhniu and Welsh Gofannon. Both names mean "smith," and in both cases we are dealing with gods of the forge. On the other hand, we have Manannán mac Lir from Ireland and Manawydan mab Llyr from Wales. Although the names are virtually identical, the surviving stories surrounding these two gods are rather different, and they emerge as two distinct mythological personalities. So, a similar-sounding name may indicate a connection...but then, again, it may not.

Mention of Goibhniu/Gofannon brings up another point. This is an example of a deity with a fairly specialized function, and we find some other goddesses and gods of this sort in the Celtic tradition. This seems particularly to be the case with the group of Irish deities known as the Túatha Dé Danann ("Tribes of the Goddess Dana") and the Welsh deities called Plant Dôn ("Children of Dôn"). Most Celtic deities, however, tend to be generalists rather than specialists. By and large, it is a mistake to pigeonhole a Celtic deity as, for example, "goddess of love" or "sun god." The ancient Celts seem to have preferred a deity who was good at or interested in a range of things. So a god with solar associations might at the same time be a god of crafts and martial prowess. Even Goibhniu, primarily a smith, has another role in Irish mythology: He's the fellow who brews the ale for the Otherworld feast!

Sometimes the functions of Celtic deities are quite broad, and one deity may be complementary to another. This is especially obvious in the case of divine couples. In sculpture and inscriptions from Gaul and Britain and in much of the recorded mythology, we see a goddess and a god paired. Sometimes they come together just once, for ritual purposes; sometimes they are ongoing partners. In general terms, many of these couples can be seen as a union between the goddess of the land and the god of the tribe. The goddess tends to represent nature and fertility, with the god representing culture and protection. If the god (or hero) is a king (or would-be king), his goddess-partner is a manifestation or symbol of sovereignty— the power of just rule in relationship with the land. In every instance, these couples are in equal, harmonious partnership, joined together to promote the holistic well-being of land and people.

Finally, as you read or listen to stories of the goddesses and gods, here are a few things to keep in mind about mythology in general. The same myth can operate at different levels and can be interpreted in a variety of ways—all of which may be true, all at the same time. The meaning of a myth is not literal. Myth is not history, but poetry. Myths speak in the language of symbols, telling stories that reveal the mysteries to "those with ears to hear," but concealing the mysteries from others. And most of our Celtic myths have come down to us imperfectly preserved, making it even more necessary for us to look for the hidden meaning within the words.

Chapter 3

What This Book Does and Doesn't Do

With hundreds of deities and centuries of tradition, with an endless variety of stories to tell and limitless ways to revere the various Celtic deities and heroes, the subject of this book could fill an entire library. Naturally, an introductory volume needs to be focused. So, in this chapter we'd like to briefly discuss our objectives—and, perhaps just as important, discuss a few things that we are *not* attempting to cover. The chapter ends with a brief overview of different theories about the nature of the deities. Rather than tell you *what* to believe, we're offering a variety of *possible* beliefs, leaving it up to you to decide how you think about the Celtic gods and goddesses—in accord with your own experience or ideas about the cosmos.

Our Goals

We have three primary goals:

To introduce you to a variety of the most important and interesting Celtic deities. Yes, of the hundreds of Celtic goddesses and gods, most were localized spirits specific to just one region or community. Others achieved greater prominence, with a few truly becoming "pan-Celtic" and venerated throughout the ancient Celtic world. For this book, we have taken a small number of the best-known or most fascinating deities from different parts of the Celtic world and present them through stories and spiritual reflection. Our goal is to help you gain a sense of some of the "key players" in the tradition. But keep in mind—fewer than 10 percent of the known Celtic deities are covered here.

To present the deities through stories and lore associated with them. Many books on Pagan gods and goddesses (Celtic or otherwise) provide abstract lists of characteristics or magical powers associated with various deities. This can be useful for planning rituals or developing magical workings, but such lists do little to help us grow spiritually in relation to the deities. Historically, people learned about the old gods and goddesses through storytelling—hearing about the deities' exploits and mighty acts through tales told while sitting around the fire. In today's media-dominated world, such traditional storytelling practices are rapidly dying out. While a book can never replace a true storyteller, we have made efforts to present the deities in the most traditional way we can: by recounting, whenever possible, one or more stories associated with each one.

To offer ideas and suggestions on how you can foster a more intimate relationship with the deities in your own life. It's fascinating to learn about the gods and goddesses and enlightening to learn some of the old stories from the myths and lore. However, this book intends to help today's Wiccans, Druids, and other Neo-Pagans actually grow spiritually in relation to the deities. Therefore, this book is more than just a compendium of information. It is intended as a manual for devotional and magical growth. We believe that deepening your mystical relationship with each of these deities can have marvelous spiritual and psychological benefits. Therefore, we've written this book in a manner that we hope will help you foster genuine intimacy with the deities. We invite you to approach them as living entities who can make our lives better, stronger, happier, and more fulfilling—with or without our magical efforts.

Now, here are some points to consider in terms of what we are *not* providing for you in this book:

We offer no spells, lists of magical attributes, or tables of correspondences. Plenty of magical and Wiccan books provide scads of information on different deities—from what their animal totems are, to the best time of day to work spells related to them, to the best herbs to use in ritual with them. Such fact-intensive books can easily be misunderstood: They can give the impression that the gods and goddesses exist strictly as some sort of psychic or spiritual resource to be exploited in the pursuit of magical power. We'd like to suggest a different approach to the gods. Authentic Celtic spirituality is not primarily based on casting spells or using magic to always get our way in life (even though there is a legitimate place for magic in Celtic wisdom). We want to emphasize not the magic or the spellcraft, but the spirituality and mysticism of Celtic Paganism. In other words, we invite you to let magic take a backseat to enlightenment. By getting to know the stories of the deities and by considering how to invite them into your daily life, you can find spiritual meaning through divine intimacy— what mystics of many different ages and traditions have called union with the divine. It's almost like taking the time to get to know a person you're falling in love with. Thankfully, as Pagans, we don't have to approach the gods from a position of self-denial or overblown humility; on the contrary, we believe the gods and goddesses wish to honor, enjoy, and love us as much as they desire honor, joy, and love *from us*. By the way, just because there are no tables of magical attributes in this book doesn't mean you can't use it to help create rituals or spells. Indeed, each chapter is filled with magically relevant information. We've just arranged it in such a way that the mysticism (intimacy with the gods) comes before the magic (conducting business with the gods).

We're not providing you with an "academic" approach to the deities. Make no mistake: We believe in honoring the old Celtic stories and traditions, and so we have made every effort to provide accurate and detailed information based on ancient teachings and lore. But scholarship is not our primary focus. If you want an in-depth academic survey of the Celtic gods and goddesses, please consult the bibliography to get some ideas of useful books to explore. You could easily make learning about the Celtic deities a lifetime project (we certainly have!). Here, rather than provide exhaustive details, we've endeavored to give you just enough information on each deity to help you grow spiritually in relation to them—and, hopefully, to inspire you to further study elsewhere.

We don't tell you what to believe. This is actually the main thing this book doesn't do. Since most Neo-Pagans are uncomfortable with dogmas or any kind of externally imposed beliefs, it is hardly appropriate for us, as authors, to present our beliefs as authoritative or absolute. There is no consensus (within the Pagan community or beyond) as to what the ancient Celts believed, or even how they practiced their spirituality. Because the written sources for the gods and goddesses only date back to Roman or Christian times, they may not provide us with the most accurate understanding of primal Celtic beliefs. Ancient historians such as Strabo even suggested that the earliest Celts did not have "gods" and "goddesses" at all, but simply worshipped nature.

The Deities and the Question of Belief

We who are interested in Celtic spirituality must make do with the limited information, mythology, and imagery that is available. Out of the fragmentary data from the past, we seek to create a faith that is meaningful for the present and future. But what *can* we believe regarding the Celtic gods and goddesses? Are they "real" in the sense that Christians believe the Holy Spirit is real? Or are they metaphors? Where do the gods live—does the Otherworld exist only in our minds (as in the Jungian concept of the collective unconscious), or is there some sort of objective spiritual reality that would continue to exist even if every human being died?

Do the Celtic gods and goddesses represent aspects of a single Divine Being? Or of a single Lord and a single Lady, following in Dion Fortune's idea that "all the gods are one God, and all the goddesses one Goddess"? Or does Celtic spirituality make the most sense without any concept of a monistic God or God/dess, leaving only the many gods and goddesses as our "map" of the spiritual world?

These are complex questions, and because the world of Celtic spirituality has no bible, pope, or dogma, different Pagan individuals and groups are free to draw their own conclusions about Celtic cosmology, based on their interpretations of the myths and folklore, their understanding of history and archaeology, and their personal experience. For this reason, instead of declaring one "correct" approach to understanding the gods and goddesses, we'd like to offer seven different ways to think about the Celtic deities, leaving it up to you to decide which of these perspectives makes the most sense for you.

The Animistic Approach: The gods and goddesses personify forces within nature. Brigit and fire; Rhiannon and horses; Cernunnos and stags; Manannán and the ocean. So many Celtic deities have a powerful mythic connection to one or more aspects of the natural world. Perhaps to the Celts, the gods were simply metaphors for the true seat of divinity: the world in which we live. It's an idea in keeping with Strabo's observation about the religion of our Celtic ancestors.

The Archetypal Approach: The gods and goddesses are symbolic rather than "real." This theory regards the deities of the Celts (and of all other cultures) as strictly ideas, concepts, or images. Ceridwen and the Dagda are no more real than Frodo or Harry Potter. This doesn't make them useless, for even a good story can teach us about values, about psychology, about the dynamics of human behavior. Indeed, the importance of the myths and legends in archetypal terms is that each deity symbolizes virtues or skills or emotions, and, as we learn their stories, we learn about the qualities that make life worth living. This approach sees the gods and goddesses as metaphorical doorways into the riches of the human imagination.

The Transpersonal Approach: The gods and goddesses represent powerful energies within the collective unconscious, or are thought-forms created by human psychic energy. If the gods and goddesses are purely products of the human mind, that doesn't mean they are just make-believe. Humankind barely understands the full extent of psychic and spiritual power available to us through our minds; such phenomena as telepathy, intuition, prophetic dreams, and past-life recall suggest that our individual consciousnesses may be more intricately linked than science currently can measure or comprehend. Within that vast network of collective mind, perhaps the gods and goddesses receive enough energy to exist independent of any one person's will. Seen this way, the deities are "other" than us and can relate to us, even if only through the mysteries of the mind.

The Euhemerist Approach: The gods and goddesses were originally humans whose extraordinary deeds came to be regarded as divine. Named after an ancient Greek philosopher, this theory of polytheism sees mythic gods and heroes as having originally been mortal men and women who, over the ages, came to be regarded as having miraculous powers. Consider how both Christianity and Buddhism are based on the life and teachings of a person believed to have existed many centuries ago: Jesus and Siddhartha. But we know nothing about what these men were truly like, for both of them have been eclipsed by mythology and legend that have grown up around them. In the eyes of his followers, Jesus was an *avatar*—a god who entered into history by incarnating in human form. Siddhartha, by contrast, was a *buddha*—a mortal human who, by dint of his own efforts, achieved pure enlightenment (and, some would say, divine power). In thinking about the Celtic gods and goddesses, we need to remember that they could be the ancestral Celtic equivalent of buddhas and avatars—men and women who, in some form, manifested the energy of divinity.

The Monistic Approach: The deities are aspects of a single deity, or a single Lord/Lady duality. Some Neo-Pagans approach deities as existing beyond the power and scope of human ability. In other words, the gods do not need us to exist. But then, how do they exist? One theory, made famous by the British occultist Dion Fortune, is that all gods and goddesses are aspects of a single deity (or pair of deities), similar to the way that every facet is an aspect of a single jewel. Kind of like Joseph Campbell's "hero with a thousand faces," the "One Spirit" is revealed to us as an infinite number of individual deities, each of whom embody one or more qualities that are all subsumed within that single Spirit. In this view, whenever we relate to deities like Rhiannon or Lugh, we are actually revering the One Spirit through a particular mythical form.

The Henotheistic Approach: The gods and goddesses are distinct spiritual entities who exist as highly evolved beings, but not to be identified as the single, ultimate source/deity. Some people find the monistic approach to Pagan spirituality to be too simple. After all, the gods and goddesses have radically different personalities, values, behaviors, and relate to each other in different ways. Many don't even like each other! Isn't it a little ingenuous to simply lump them all together as part of a single "Source"? For this reason, some Neo-Pagans are henotheistic: They venerate the gods or goddesses of their choosing, regarding the various deities as separate and distinct entities, but do not deny the existence of other gods (including, perhaps, an ultimate god or god/goddess). They might see the ultimate as an impersonal force, à la *Star Wars*, or as an overarching mother figure, as, for example, the Irish goddess Anu is sometimes seen. This ultimate source provides the cosmological ground in which the other deities live and function—as independent beings with divine abilities.

The Polytheistic Approach: The gods and goddesses are real, distinct spiritual entities, existing with us in a cosmos without a single ultimate source or deity. This theory holds that a committee, not a dictator, runs the universe. Seen this way, there's no such thing as a single, omniscient, omnipotent god, but all the gods represent a variety of powers and abilities. The gods are real, they exist separate from humanity, and no one knows how they came to be, or if they're immortal, or exist in physical form somewhere "other" than our world. Within polytheism there can be a variety of theories about the origin of the universe, the nature of the gods, and the ultimate meaning of life. But all this speculation begins with the assumption that either there is no ultimate god, or that it is meaningless or philosophically self-contradictory to even talk about such an entity.

A reminder: We take no stand as to which approach to the deities is the right or best one. We also recognize that there are other possible approaches, and that these perspectives are not necessarily mutually exclusive. We've tried to write this book in a way that would make it useful to everyone interested in Celtic spirituality, regardless of which theological model(s) you follow. Believe according to the dictates of your conscience, and we hope the information in the pages that follow will be helpful for your ongoing spiritual journey.

Thinking Polytheistically

As we journey into the world of the goddesses, gods, heroines, and heroes, here are a few ideas to keep in mind:

- ❧ In polytheism, no one god or goddess is assumed to be all-powerful or all-knowing.

- ❧ Different gods and goddesses may have different degrees of power or ability.

- ❧ Morality varies among the deities just as it does among humans. No one deity is "purely good" or "purely evil."

- ❧ Because they are gods and not mortals, we can assume they are more powerful than us and do not need us. But that's like saying we don't need dogs and cats. Just as we humans get great pleasure and joy out of our pets and can learn from them, so the deities may derive greater or lesser benefits from our honoring and veneration of them. For this reason, we can assume the deities like having us around and take an interest in us and in our spiritual devotion to them.

- ❧ The relationship between deities and mortals is based on exchange. They don't owe us anything (and neither do we owe them anything). But we can offer "sacrifices" such as praise, devotion, or ritual, and they in turn offer us their blessings or divine assistance. Like all healthy relationships, our connection with the gods and goddesses is based on give-and-take.

Part Two:

Goddesses
and Heroines

Chapter 4

The Mothers: Threefold Soul of the Earth

To the ancient Celts, the land on which they lived was holy, full of the spirit of the divine. The landscape, with its hills and streams, was the visible manifestation of sacred power, the outer garment of the spirit that dwelled within. This land, this spirit, was the great bearer and nurturer of the people. And so the land was often called Mother.

In the Celtic tradition, what is powerful once is all the more powerful in threes. The ancient Celts (like many peoples) invested certain numbers with mystical significance, and the number three was primary among these. We may never fully understand all that it meant to the Celts, but we can make educated guesses about much of its symbolism. As the sum of the first two numbers, three signifies completion. The mating of female and male produce a third being, making three the number of manifestation. Time is perceived as a triad of past, present, and future, and so three symbolizes the unity of time—as it does of space (underworld, earth, and the heavens; land, sea, and sky; above, below, and here; etc.). The number three indicates exponentially increased power: any image, utterance, or action is magically intensified by being repeated three times.

All of these ideas—and more, no doubt—are present in the triple image of the Mothers, perhaps the most widely honored deities in the ancient Celtic world. The geographic range of their worship is indicated by an inscription found in Winchester, England, that makes a dedication to the "Italian, German, Gaulish, and British Mothers" (Miranda Green, *Celtic Goddesses*, p. 106). It also appears that the Mothers were revered by all segments of society—by women and men, by rich and poor. Even Roman soldiers stationed in Celtic areas worshipped the Mothers.

In Roman-ruled Gaul and Britain, the Mothers were frequently portrayed as three women side by side. They hold emblems of abundance, fertility, and nurture, such as cornucopias, loaves of bread, trays of fruit, and babies. Sometimes the women are identical, or nearly so. Sometimes there are subtle differences between them, or even quite distinctive variations—in their hairstyles, clothing, or emblems (although these generally all keep to the same theme). A particularly tender relief from Gaul, full of the imagery of maternal TLC, shows three seated goddesses, each with her right breast uncovered, ready for nursing. One holds a sponge and basin, the middle one has ready a swaddling cloth or towel, and the third cradles a swaddled baby in her arms.

Occasionally, age differences are noticeable in portrayals of the Mothers: there may be one older woman with two younger women, or two older with one younger. This age difference appears also in a number of images from southwestern Gaul that show the Mothers as two women, not three. But whether there are two or three Mothers, if there is a contrast in the ages of the figures, it is almost always between youth and maturity. It is very rare to find Celtic images that portray youth, maturity, *and* old age; the Maiden-Mother-Crone triad popularized by Robert Graves in *The White Goddess* was not, it appears, a major archetype among the Celts.

Inscriptions to the Mothers address them as Matronae, Matres, or Deae Matres ("Goddess Mothers"). Sometimes the Mothers have "surnames," such as the Matres Domesticae honored at several locations in Britain. *Domesticae* in these cases was probably used to mean "of the homeland." Matres Brittanicae ("of Britain") and Matres Gallicae ("of Gaul") are also known. In other instances, the Mothers' surname identified them with a more particular people or place. For example, the Matres Treverae were the Mothers of the Treveri tribe (who lived near modern Trier, Germany); the Nemausicae were worshipped at Nemausus (modern-day Nîmes, France), where they were also closely associated with the town's healing spring.

In fact, the Mothers were frequently revered at healing springs, such as the famous one at Bath, known in ancient times as Aquae Sulis ("The Waters of Sulis"). Here the triple Mothers were known as Suleviae or Matres Suleviae. The Suleviae were worshipped in two other locations in Britain and also in Gaul, Germany, and Hungary. The root of *Suleviae* (and *Sulis*) is related to a Celtic word for "sun." Because many healing springs were hot springs, these names may express the idea that the goddesses of the earth from which the springs well up hold and dispense the heat and healing power of the sun.

A link between the Mothers and healing was also made by the appearance of dogs in some images—in both the Roman and Celtic cultures, dogs were associated with healing. In addition, they sometimes had a connection with death and the Otherworld. And some images of the Mothers do appear to have associations not only with the beginning and fullness of life, but with the end of life as well. In the Burgundy region of France, for example, the Mothers are sometimes portrayed with such objects as balance-scales, scrolls, spinning equipment, and steering oars—attributes that belonged to the Roman world's goddesses of Fate and Fortune. In Burgundy, too, images of the Mothers have been found in graves and caves.

When the earth is regarded as a mother, burial in the earth (which was commonly practiced by the ancient Celts) can be seen as a return to the womb. This, of course, is preparation for rebirth. As goddesses of both birth and death, the Mothers—with their triple symbolism of unity—show that there is really no difference between the two. Birth is death to the Otherworld; death is birth *into* the Otherworld. Standing between these two points—like the images of the Mothers that show a young woman between two older ones—is our life on earth (and, on the other side of the veil, our life in the Otherworld).

The Mothers and the Fairy Folk

These goddesses seem to have lived on in Welsh folk tradition as Y Mamau, "The Mothers"—one of the names for the Fairy Folk. A variant on this name is Bendith y Mamau, "The Blessing of the Mothers." Welsh fairies, like the Mothers in many instances, have traditionally been associated with caves and springs (as well as lakes). They also have strong links to childbirth and young children—although often not to the earthly benefit of human families. New mothers, babies, and children were thought very vulnerable to being stolen by the fairies—but then, this can be seen as a reflection of the fragility of life and, particularly, the uncertainty of maternal and infant survival in earlier times. This aspect of Y Mamau would certainly be in keeping with the Mothers' aspect as deities who watched over birth and death.

If we regard the Fairy Folk as "nature spirits"—or, more precisely, spiritual beings or presences that inhabit the natural world—we see an even stronger link to the ancient Mothers. We might, therefore, look to some of the Celtic fairy lore for ideas of ways to honor the Mothers. For instance, Welsh fairies were well known for holding cleanliness and good manners in high esteem. Well, that sounds very mundane (and very motherly!), but consider the wider applications and implications. Is your spirit clean—or only your house? You may keep your own yard neat and tidy—but away from home, are you careful not to litter; do you clean up other people's litter when you can? If you visit a sacred site, you leave only offerings that will quickly biodegrade, right? The more you think about it, the more you see that cleanliness and manners are closely related. Both are matters of respect: to yourself, to others, to the environment, and to the deities. Showing respect, or at least courtesy, is a way of recognizing the divine potential in everyone and everything.

Wherever you are, make it a point to notice the divine in nature—even if the only greenery you have close at hand is a potted plant. Realize that the place where you live has its own Mothers. If you pay attention, you can see them in every curve of the landscape; you can taste their love in the breads and fruits you eat; you can feel their warmth in the water you shower in. The Mothers are with you, in all the blessings on your life.

Occasions For Honoring the Mothers

In the ancient world, the Mothers were sometimes addressed as Iunones, connecting them with the Roman concept of the Iuno, a woman's guardian spirit. On some images, too, the Mothers were portrayed wearing crescent-moon amulets. For these reasons, many women may feel drawn to honor the Mothers during their "moon time," or period. Those images that portray the Mothers as both young and mature women also suggest that these goddesses would be good to call on for a girl's coming of age. And of course, the Mothers are ideal deities for pregnant women to turn to.

Remember, though, that the Mothers were not just women's deities; they could be approached by anyone. After all, everyone has an interest in the Mothers' abundance. And every one of us owes our existence not only to our human mother, but also to Mother Earth. Mother's Day would be an ideal occasion for honoring the Mothers in some fashion; even sending a Mother's Day card to your mom or to another significant female figure in your life can be an act of conscious devotion to the Mothers. Earth Day, too, could be considered a holiday dedicated to the Mothers.

On an everyday basis, we might consider composing a grace to say at meals to specifically honor the Mothers' gifts of life. Another good time to pray to the Mothers is just before going to sleep or just after waking up—or both—for the cycle of waking and sleeping mirrors the cycle of birth and death. In this analogy, we live our life on earth during the day and, when we are sleeping and dreaming, we live our life in the Otherworld. The gateways between those two lives are the birth/death of waking up and the birth/death of falling asleep.

Sooner or later, each of us faces death itself. It is nearly impossible to go through life without losing a friend, a pet, a family member, a co-worker.... Over time, most of us experience multiple losses. On sad occasions such as these, it is good to be mindful of the Mothers, with their reassurance that death is only a brief passage—a temporary separation. And when, eventually, we face our own death, we can do so knowing that the loving arms of the Mothers await us in the Otherworld.

Chapter 5

Anu and
the River Goddesses

In the Celtic world, water and sacrifice often seem to go together. At the headwaters of the Seine River in France, archaeologists have discovered numerous votive offerings, many carved in wood and symbolizing a variety of physical ailments—probably representing the complaints of the supplicants who worshipped there. Large hordes of silver offerings have been found in other rivers, notably the Thames in England. To this day, coins are left at holy wells in the Celtic world.

With so much evidence for ritual activity of this nature, it seems reasonable to assume that our Celtic ancestors were particularly committed to venerating the gods or goddesses associated with rivers and other bodies of water. True enough, many deities have such associations—a fact echoed in the number of Celtic rivers and goddesses with shared or similar names. Boann and the Boyne River; Danu and the Danube; Sinann and the Shannon; Brigantia and the Brent River: These are some of the better-known deity-river connections.

In Ireland, both the Shannon and the Boyne are connected to mythic stories about goddesses and sacred wells. Sinann—the granddaughter of the great god of the sea, Lir—learns that wisdom can be found at the sacred Well of Connla. No one really knows who Connla was, but the reputation of his well extended far and wide; nine hazel trees, whose nuts were sources of esoteric knowledge and inspiration, surrounded it. When one of the nuts fell into the water, a salmon swimming in the well would eat it, gaining one red spot on its body for each of the nuts it had consumed.

So here at Connla's Well, three symbols—hazelnut, salmon, and the well itself—formed a triad of divine wisdom. Sinann wanted this wisdom for herself, even though the only people allowed access to the well were Nechtan (a shadowy figure whose name may have an origin similar to *Neptune*, implying a water god) and his servants. Sinann approached the well in secret, disregarding the prohibition—and with disastrous results. Instead of drinking the water, catching the fish, or eating the nuts, she found that the well reacted with anger to her unauthorized presence—the water rose up and rushed over her, drowning her and carrying her spirit to the ocean. The river that resulted became known as the Shannon.

On the eastern side of Ireland, strikingly similar tales were told to explain the origin of the River Boyne. This time, the goddess involved is Nechtan's wife, Boann. Her name comes from an Indo-European root that seems to mean "White Cow Goddess," suggesting that originally she was a goddess of livestock and agriculture. But the tales that are told of her echo the story of Sinann: Her husband is the guardian of the mythical Well of Segais, surrounded by nine hazel trees and in which lived the mystical salmon of knowledge. Like her sister-goddess to the west, Boann defies the taboo against visiting the well. In some of the legends told about her, the well rushes her three times, each time wounding her—the first time blinding her in one eye, then maiming one hand, and finally harming one leg. She becomes a shamanistic figure of supernatural insight, but to little avail—for again, the well rises up and rushes after her, drowning her and creating the Boyne River.

The stories are so similar that they doubtless have some common origin; together they testify to the importance of the goddess energy found within the waters of a flowing river. Indeed, one of the earliest—if not *the* earliest—of Celtic goddesses is Danu ("The Flowing One"), who gave her name not only to the great Danube River, but also to the tribe of Irish deities and magical heroes, the Túatha Dé Danann ("Tribes of the Goddess Dana"). She is in all likelihood the same as a goddess who appears in the Sanskrit scriptures of India: In the Rig-Veda, Danu is the name of a river goddess similar to Sinann and Boann. Variants of her name include Dana and Anu—the name of an Irish goddess from the southwest part of the country who, in the Middle Ages, was identified as the mother of the gods. In Wales, the goddess Dôn, as an unseen mother of deities, appears to play a role similar to Danu's.

Danu is a hidden and mysterious figure in Ireland, appearing not so much as an active character in the myths, but rather as a shadowy presence, known by her name or through her children. Presumably, all of the Túatha Dé can trace their lineage back to her, although some figures are specifi-cally identified as Anu's children—most notably the three sons of Tuireann (Brian, Iuchair, and Iucharba). Some traditions hold that the mother of Tuireann's children was in fact Brigit, leading to the speculation that Brigit and Danu/Anu may in fact be the same goddess. As we will see in Chapter 6, Brigit is actually a title (the "exalted one"), and because she has an associa-tion both with the fertility of the land (a characteristic of Anu) and the sacredness of water (a characteristic of Danu), it's not an unreasonable theory. According to Irish scholar Dáithí Ó hÓgáin, other Irish goddesses (such as the Morrigán) whose names are actually titles may in fact be different aspects of Danu as the great mother goddess of the land.

Notice I said "of the land." Part of the mystery of Danu is that, although she appears to originate as an ancient river goddess, at some point in Irish history she seemed to make a transition from Danu of the sacred waters to Anu of the sacred land. The *d* in her name survives only in the name of her people: Túatha Dé Danann. Meanwhile, two lovely mountain peaks in County Kerry are known as Dá Chích nAnann—the "two paps of Anu," the goddess so at one with the land that the hills are a sign of her nurturing presence. Anu's name in Irish means "wealth," suggesting that the land is the source and the fact of all true prosperity. The Irish province of Munster paid particular homage to her, although at least one medieval manuscript refers to Ireland in its entirety as Iath nAnann, or the "Land of Anu."

Deities of Nature

Boann, Sinann, Anu, and Danu ultimately share one essential feature: They are all goddesses known to us through their identity with nature, whether through the sacred waters of a specific river or simply through the holiness of the land itself. The transition of Danu from primeval river god-dess to the more generalized goddess of the land as Anu suggests that Celtic spirituality, as it developed, became increasingly conscious of the universality of spirit—the deities are more than just denizens of this river or that mountain, but truly embody a cosmic dimension. This means that, for us today, Celtic spirituality can have universal relevance, regardless of where we live or of which spirits inhabit the land and waterways of our region. Of course, this universality does not negate the profound connec-tion that so many Celtic deities have with a specific location. While Anu symbolizes the entirety of the land of Ireland (a role she shares with other goddesses, including Ériu, for whom Ireland is named), Sinann and Boann remain the regional goddesses of their respective rivers.

As nature deities, Anu or the river goddesses may seem abstract or distant to the vast majority of modern people who live in suburban or urban settings. Of course, nature (including rivers) is just as much a part of city life as it is present in the country, but it may take conscious commitment for 21st-century urbanites to meaningfully connect with these ancient earth spirits. Furthermore, given how little we really know about these goddesses, there's not much material in the tradition from which we can construct rituals or other devotional practices. Therefore, we could see the worship of these deities as a kind of *tabula rasa*—a blank page on which we can create new traditions and rituals. There is nothing wrong with developing innovative ways of venerating ancient gods and goddesses, as long as we are honest about what we are doing. Tradition, after all, is a living thing, and the only way to keep Celtic (or any) spirituality alive and vibrant is to experiment with new ways to help the tradition evolve.

Honoring the Nature Goddesses

Here, then, are some "new ideas" for honoring Danu and the other goddesses featured in this chapter, in ways that are relevant to the 21st century. More than anything else, to honor Anu or the river goddesses, begin by revering the ground you walk on—literally. If you don't know the river(s) nearest to your home, find out where they are and investigate whether there are environmental organizations dedicated to preserving the river's ecosystem (we live near the Chattahoochee River in Georgia, where an excellent group called the Chattahoochee Riverkeepers works hard to protect the river and raise public awareness about environmental issues). Meanwhile, in your rituals and meditations, contemplate how the soil, the landscape, the hills and mountains, and especially the rivers or any other bodies of water near you all have their own spirit—their own personality. Through meditation and inner journeying, you can develop a sense of connection to these mighty entities. An important reminder: These spirits will be native to your homeland, so unless you happen to live in Ireland or some other place traditionally associated with Danu, you are likely to be encountering spirits who are different from the ones we've told you about here. *That is okay.* Celtic mysticism does not require you to venerate only the gods or goddesses who were mentioned in the old Irish or Welsh myths.

It's far better for you to make a spiritual connection to the divine spirits of your own bioregion—and the features of your environment that they embody or represent. Remember the saying *Charity begins at home*? Well, so does Celtic spirituality. Maybe the gods and goddesses of your homeland are not figures from the Celtic tradition—but if you take the time to spiritually connect with them, or to honor them, you are practicing a spiritual path that is in perfect harmony with the old Celtic ways.

How do you connect with local deities? We've already mentioned one important way: through meditation and ritual. Just remember, to take your meditation to its deepest level, you'll want to balance your inner explorations with whatever traditions and legends and lore are based in your homeland. If you live in North America, that would mean a Native American culture. Other parts of the world have their own local traditions and myths. As a follower of the Celtic path, this does not mean you are obligated to wholeheartedly adopt the spiritual practices indigenous to your homeland (indeed, many native peoples throughout the world do not appreciate non-natives adopting their spiritual practices). But do treat whatever myth and lore is connected to your region with humility and respect. Out of that respectful approach, learn what you can about the spiritual traditions of your home. In doing so, you will be simultaneously honoring those traditions, as well as the nature-based deities of the Celts.

Other ways to honor Anu and her sisters include practicing water conservation, drinking plenty of water every day, going swimming, and placing a small fountain in your home (ideally on or near your altar, if you have one). Finally, do what you can to cultivate wisdom in your life—as long as it doesn't involve visiting a forbidden well!

Chapter 6

Brigit:
The Exalted One

rigit has become one of the most celebrated goddesses in the contemporary Pagan, Wiccan, and feminist spiritual world. Numerous statues and pendants of her can be found in New Age shops; many Websites are devoted to her; and *Brigit* (or such variants as *Brigid* and *Brighid*) are popular magical names adopted by those who feel a particular kinship with her. There are many reasons why she has achieved such latter-day popularity. As a goddess of poetry, magic, and healing, her personality appeals to many Pagans. Her survival as a "saint" after the coming of Christianity to Ireland points to how resilient goddess spirituality is, even under less than ideal conditions. Because Brigit is associated with the Gaelic spring festival of Imbolc, one of the holidays observed by many Neo-Pagans, she seems to warrant status as a major goddess, even by world standards. Mara Freeman argues that Brigit is probably the nearest figure in Celtic mythology to a Great Mother goddess. All in all, she's become a genuine Neo-Pagan superstar. Given what her name means ("the exalted one" or "she who rises"), this is perhaps not surprising.

But there's a bit of irony in Brigit's revival. Many other goddesses (and gods) in world mythology have much more information available about their nature, appearance, personality, and mythic deeds. Isis from Egypt, Persephone and Demeter from Greece, Freyja from Norse tradition, and even Rhiannon from Wales are examples of goddesses of whom we know much, much more than we do about Brigit. Like so many of the figures from the Celtic tradition, our knowledge of Brigit is somewhat speculative, largely pieced together from a number of fragmentary or minor sources. In fact, most of what we think of as describing Brigit actually comes from four different sources: mythological information about an Irish goddess named Brig, a brief reference to a threefold goddess from a medieval Irish dictionary, the folklore traditions of Gaelic Ireland and Scotland, and the many legends and miraculous stories associated with Brigit in her latter-day guise as an Irish Christian saint.

The History of Brigit

Brigit of Irish myth. Irish lore names Brig as a daughter of the Dagda, the overarching father god of the Pagan Irish (see Chapter 14). But the stories about this goddess are murky; she is sometimes equated with Dana, the mother goddess for whom the Túatha Dé Danann are named. Although a goddess of the Túatha Dé Danann, Brig married Bres, a royal figure from the Túatha Dé's enemies, the Fomorians. Because of this, she embodied diplomacy and worked for peace between the warring tribes. She had a son with Bres named Rúadán, who eventually was killed in battle by the smith god Goibhniu. Rúadán's death provoked Brig to wail in lament, which became known as *keening*. As a diplomat, the sorrowful mother of a fallen warrior, and the inventor of keening, Brig began her long reputation as a peacemaker and peacekeeper.

Brigit of medieval memory. In the 10th century, an Irish bishop named Cormac compiled a glossary in which Brigit is mentioned. He describes her as a goddess particularly of poetry and of seers: "a woman of wisdom…a goddess whom poets adored, because her protection was very great and very famous." In ancient Ireland, poetry and seership were interlinked arts. The Irish word *filidecht* refers to what we would call oracular poetry, or the poetry of psychic inspiration. To be a poet was to be a diviner, and Brigit oversaw both arts. Cormac goes on to say that Brigit has two sisters, both of whom are also named Brigit: Brigit the goddess of healing, herbalism, and midwives; and Brigit the goddess of smiths. The three sisters might properly be seen as three faces of a unified triple goddess. It is here that we find Brigit's association with fire, which would survive so ceremoniously into the Christian world. As goddess of poetry, she ruled over the *imbas*, the illuminating fires of poetic inspiration: the "fire in the head." As a healing goddess she ruled over the hearth fire, and as a goddess of technology she ruled over the smith's forge. Here we see that traditional Celtic appreciation of the unity of outer and inner realms: This fire goddess governs both the inner fires of the soul as well as the physical fires of hearth and forge. Incidentally, smithcraft, while ostensibly a technological skill, functions as a metaphor for magical power. So when Cormac describes Brigit as a goddess of the forge, we can infer that she would also have been seen as a goddess ruling over the magical arts.

Brigit of Christian legend. Speaking of magic, nowhere does Brigit's magical prowess more firmly appear than in the legends and tales associated with the Christian saint Brigit. Although biographies of a powerful and pious nun of the fifth and sixth centuries appeared in Ireland as early as the eighth century, today many scholars question whether Saint Brigit ever existed as a mortal human woman. Indeed, religious historian James Frazer dismissed Saint Brigit as "an old goddess of fertility, disguised in a threadbare Christian cloak." Certainly, many of the attributes associated with the Pagan goddess also appear connected to the Christian saint. The saint has numerous miracle stories in which she causes butter and milk to multiply in abundance; compare this to the goddess who is linked with the Pagan festival of Imbolc, an agricultural holiday that coincided with the lactation of ewes. We've already seen how the goddess Brigit became linked with peacemaking; Saint Brigit plays a similar role, at one point giving her father's sword to a pauper and instructing him to sell it in order to raise money to feed his family. Metaphorically, such a story conveys a strong message of "bread before arms." As a goddess of spring, Brigit rules over abundance and increase, qualities that dance throughout the legends told of the Christian saint. Indeed, much of the character and charm of Brigit today comes to us through the saint: she turned water into beer, tricked kings into setting prisoners free, and at other times tricked kings out of land; she gouged her eye out to avoid an unwanted suitor, only to miraculously heal herself as soon as the suitor departed.

Even the stories surrounding her birth are mythical and hint at her divine origin. She was the daughter of a Pagan nobleman and a Christian slave woman, born exactly at dawn as her mother stepped over a threshold: neither Pagan nor Christian, neither slave nor free, neither born indoors nor outdoors, neither born at day nor at night. It was said that when she was born, her mother was carrying a pail of milk; it was also said that, as a baby, Brigit would only eat milk and cheese from a particular white cow with red ears. These colors are traditional symbols of the Otherworld. One final note about Saint Brigit: Legend holds that she was consecrated as a bishop. Indeed, Irish iconography to this day portrays Brigit as a nun holding a bishop's crozier. Even if Saint Brigit really existed, it seems implausible that the Christian Church would have stood for her functioning as a bishop. In other words, this folklore points to the powerful role she played—and continues to play—as a symbol of feminine spiritual authority, even within the patriarchal limitations of the Christian religion.

Brigit of Gaelic folklore. And now we come to Brigit as she has survived in folklore, particularly in Ireland and the Highlands of Scotland. With the triumph of Christianity, the folklore concerning Brigit generally depicts her as a saint, but the symbolism surrounding her (and her sacred holiday—for the Catholic feast of Saint Brigit, February 1, corresponds to the Pagan celebration of Imbolc) strongly points to her Pagan origins. Folklore celebrates Brigit as a figure of healing and protection who is ceremoniously invited into the house on the eve of February 1—the traditional beginning of spring. On this night, she is said to travel throughout the land, accompanied by her white cow, and people would leave food offerings for her, as well as straw on the ground for her to kneel on when offering her blessings (and, presumably, for the cow to munch on). Brigit is associated with dandelions; snowdrops; cows and other livestock; oyster-catchers; and healing, especially of headaches. In some Scottish traditions she is believed to be held prisoner from Samhain to Imbolc by the Cailleach (the crone of winter); one tradition holds that she is rescued by Oenghus, the Gaelic god of youth and love (see Chapter 17). Another tradition holds that Brigit is, herself, the Cailleach, who transforms every spring into a renewed maiden who represents the coming of light and new life.

The Tree, the Well, and the Fire

Saint Brigit is traditionally associated with the Irish town of Kildare. Immediately, we can find more links between the goddess and the saint: The Irish name for the town is Cill Dara, which means "Church of the Oak," and tradition holds that a massive oak tree lived for centuries at the top of the hill where today Saint Brigit's Cathedral stands. This tree was said to have magical powers; for example, it was impossible to rest a weapon against it (yet another sign of Brigit's role as peacemaker). According to legend, Brigit the nun established her convent in the shadow of this oak; perhaps at an earlier time the tree itself was a sacred object of Pagan veneration.

But there's more to Kildare than a giant tree. To this day, several holy wells near the town are sacred to Brigit—indeed, of the many sacred wells and springs still venerated in Ireland today, more are dedicated to Brigit than to any other figure. Given that Brigit's name can be interpreted to mean "she who rises," perhaps the water that rises from beneath the earth to break forth in a spring or a well would have in ancient times been considered sacred to her. And speaking of that which rises, Kildare is the ancient home of another "rising" element related to Brigit—fire.

According to the 12th-century writer Giraldus Cambrensis, near the sacred tree a willow hedge protected a small temple that no man was allowed to enter. Nineteen nuns tended an eternal flame that burned for Brigit within this temple. Each nun watched the flame for one day out of a 20-day cycle; on the 20th day, the flame was said to be tended by Brigit herself during her lifetime, and afterward was left untended, with the 19th nun saying at the end of her shift, "Brigit, guard your fire, this is your night." It was said that the flame never went out when left in Brigit's care, and that no ashes accumulated from the fire. From time to time, overzealous bishops would come along and suppress the flame, denouncing it as the survival of an ancient Pagan cult; but the resilient nuns would relight it as soon as possible. After the Protestant Reformation, when King Henry VIII suppressed the monasteries, the convent in Kildare was disbanded and the flame was again extinguished, apparently this time for good. But not so fast: In the early 1990s a small community of Catholic nuns dedicated to Brigit established a center called Solas Bhríde ("the light of Brigit") in Kildare, and on Imbolc 1992, the flame was relit. It burns to this day, lovingly tended by the sisters, who are perpetuating a form of devotion that may well be over 1,500 years old.

This brings us to the question of Brigit today. With the revival of interest in ancient Celtic religion in the 20th century, devotion to Brigit as a goddess has been on the rise. But Brigit remains one of the most popular Irish saints, second only to Patrick; so she continues to enjoy devotees within Christendom, as well as among Neo-Pagans.

In Kildare, Brigit's role as a peacemaker and peacekeeper is especially honored by the Brigidine Sisters, and, each February, Solas Bhríde hosts a conference on peace issues. But this is not the only attribute of Brigit that has modern relevance. As the goddess of inspiration, she is a matron of not only poetry, but also of all the arts, from literature to music to film to dance. As goddess of the forge, she can now be seen as a patroness of high technology, from computers to the Internet to pharmaceuticals. That last item also can be related to Brigit's role as a healer, who today would take an interest in all forms of wellness and healthcare, both mainstream and alternative.

We need to remember that Brigit is truly a goddess reborn. Because so much of what we know about her from ancient times is either fragmentary or filtered through Christian lenses, we need to acknowledge that devotion to Brigit in our time and for the future will include innovative ideas and new ways of thinking about Brigit or relating to her. If you want to be a devotee of Brigit, seek to nurture a connection with poetry and prophecy— for your creativity and divination will contribute to building the new roads that the goddess will walk, today and in the future.

Brigit and the Traditions of Imbolc

To venerate Brigit, start with the day most sacred to her: February 1, Imbolc. The traditions linked to this day can provide insights into how we might honor this goddess each and every day.

In the traditional areas of Ireland and Scotland, the February rituals that mark the beginning of spring are known as the Festival of Brigit. Many of the ceremonies that have survived as part of Gaelic folklore have revolved around the theme of hospitality: of welcoming the spirit of Brigit into our lives, with the protection, healing, and blessings that this implies. If we remember that, on one level, Brigit is the personification of spring, this makes perfect sense: After several dark and cold winter months, it's a wonderful thing to welcome the Spirit of Spring! And so the customs associated with the Festival of Brigit all revolve around these themes of hospitality and welcoming. Also associated with the festival are a variety of craft items that symbolize Brigit or her blessings.

Typically, on the festival's eve or sometime prior to that date, family members gather rushes to make Brigit's crosses. According to tradition, Brigit herself first made these equal-armed crosses when explaining the cross of Christ to her father on his deathbed. This story may be charming, but it's clearly mythological: Her father would have long known about the cross of Christ from Brigit's mother or from others in his household; and if Brigit were really making the cross to teach about Christ, she probably would not have made an equal-armed cross, but rather one that would more accurately reflect a crucifix. This equal-armed cross made from rushes could possibly have Pagan origins, as a symbol of the sun or the four directions. Today, though, it is mostly a symbol of Brigit herself. Traditionally, Brigit's crosses are made by family members and hung in their house, barn, and other buildings for protection.

Another craft item that more directly represents Brigit is the *brídeog*, or "young Brigit"—a doll created as an effigy of Brigit. Many *brídeog* customs exist in different parts of the British Isles; often she is made of natural materials and decorated with seashells or colored stones. In many communities, children would carry the *brídeog* from house to house, begging for treats and offering Brigit's blessings in return; meanwhile, a Scottish custom involves children creating a *brídeog* while older women make a bed or "cradle" for her to lie in. The evening before the Festival of Brigit, the girls would ceremoniously bring the *brídeog* into the house, where she would be laid in her cradle. In some localities, she would be given a wand fashioned of white wood: perhaps a symbol for her divine lover Oenghus. The *brídeog* represents divine presence and the blessings of abundance; to welcome the *brídeog* into one's house is symbolic of welcoming the goddess herself. And so the bed represents hospitality.

Another tradition involves creating a large hoop out of wheat, straw, or rope, with three or four crosses attached to it at various points around the circle. This is known as a *Crios Bríde*, or Brigit's girdle. Everyone would step through it or jump through it three times, reciting a poem similar to this: "Brigit's girdle is my girdle, the girdle with the four crosses. Arise, housewife, and go out three times. May whoever goes through my girdle be seven times better a year from now." So this simple ceremony represents rebirth (the girdle can be a metaphor for the womb) and also blessing (a blessing for being seven times better a year hence).

One last custom associated with the evening before the festival involves taking a ribbon or piece of cloth and leaving it outdoors to receive Brigit's blessing when she passes by. This item is called the *brat Bríde*, or Brigit's mantle. It is said that when it is left outside on the eve before Imbolc so that it gathers dew, it has been blessed by Brigit herself and is imbued with healing powers, especially useful for headaches and other ailments of the head. In some localities, the *brat Bríde* needs to be left outside each Imbolc for seven years in order to gain its full potency.

These ceremonies are accompanied by typical activities of celebration: making of food and sharing it with others, giving to the poor, and participating in religious rituals (whether Christian or Neo-Pagan).

Honoring Brigit Throughout the Year

One does not need to wait for Imbolc to honor Brigit. Because of her many positive qualities, including poetic and divinatory inspiration, technological prowess, healing abilities, prosperity, and peacemaking, she is a goddess most people would like to have present in their lives. Well, the first and easiest way to call Brigit in is to work to cultivate in your own life those qualities that are sacred to her. Learn a new skill; write a poem; work for your own wellness or the healing of another; share the blessings of your life with others; and work for peace and conflict resolution, whether in big or small ways. These mundane activities, if done with a sense of devotion to Brigit, will bring her into your life faster than any other act.

Many people have followed the lead of the ancient priestesses of Brigit and light a sacred flame in her honor. Indeed, several independent organizations exist to support "flamekeepers" who light a candle or other flame as a reverent reminder of Brigit's blessing and a means to ask for her continued presence. Typically, being a flamekeeper means committing to light a flame for her ceremonially once every 20 days. But some people keep a safe flame burning every day as a way of devotion to her. While safety and practical concerns are important, this is one of the simplest and most popular ways to cultivate an ongoing sense of devotion to this goddess.

Related to this would be a similar practice of venerating water or working with natural water supplies in your vicinity as "holy wells" for Brigit. Even though she is a fire goddess, she is also the goddess of waters that rise from the hidden world below. Honoring the watery aspects of Brigit can be as simple as collecting rainwater for use in your daily devotions, to running an indoor fountain with a conscious realization that it symbolizes Brigit to you, to actually finding and regularly venerating a water source near you. However a person may make choices along this line, it is valuable chiefly as a way to invoke and honor Brigit's presence.

Near Kildare, Ireland, there is a holy well dedicated to Brigit with five small standing stones in front of it. According to a guidebook written by the Brigidine Sister Rita Minehan, each of these stones represents a quality associated with Brigit: care for the earth, peacemaking, hospitality, care for the poor, and meditation. Trying to cultivate these qualities on a daily basis can be a beautiful way to keep the spirit of Brigit central in your life.

One more way to honor Brigit is to remember that Brigit's flame is not just something that burns in a spiritual center in eastern Ireland, but it is truly one of the many "fires" that burn within us: the fires of love, of passion, of creativity, of inspiration, of spiritual fervor. Nurture such fiery qualities in your own soul, and you have honored Brigit.

Chapter 7

The Morrigán: The Phantom Queen

It is said that when an Irish warrior was heading to battle, the worst omen he could possibly receive would be to see an old crone at the ford of a river, washing the bloody garments of one who had fallen in battle. Such a vision would strike fear into the heart of even the stoutest of fighting men; and if the warrior were brave (or foolish) enough to look more closely, surely what he might find would turn his blood to ice. For when the washerwoman appeared to a warrior, it generally was *his own* garments that she was cleaning.

The Washer at the Ford was but one of many ways in which the great Phantom Queen of the Irish tradition could call fear to alight in the lives of those who were touched by her deathlike grip. This frightening goddess was a shapeshifter, who could appear in many different guises, both human and animal. Various stories depict her as a crow, an eel, a heifer, and a wolf; as a seductive young temptress, a fearsome warrior queen, and a feeble old hag. Indeed, part of the paranoia that she could so effectively wreak would be the sheer terror of not knowing just in what way she would show up next.

She is called the Morrigán, and, as with many of the Celtic deities, we know her not by name, but by title: Morrigán means "Phantom Queen." Her name also appears as the Mórrígan ("Great Queen"), suggesting a possible link with Rhiannon. And sometimes she is called the Mórrígna, or the Great Queens, in the plural because more than one divine figure was subsumed beneath the wide stretch of her raven wings. She is the goddess of war, of battle, of fury; a bringer of fear and panic, and a prophet—especially when her prophecy speaks of doom or bloodshed. Yet, as the Dagda (the skillful father god) found out to his joy—and as the hero Cú Chulainn rejected to his peril—she also sported a lusty and vigorous sexuality, abundantly willing to share her pleasures with those she deemed worthy, but vicious and unforgiving when spurned.

Goddess of the Killing Rage

The Morrigán is the goddess of bloodthirstiness—of the shift in consciousness that is precipitated by rage or battle fury. "I'm so mad that I could kill somebody" is an expression of this consciousness—her consciousness. But she's also a trickster, best known for tricking Cú Chulainn into blessing her during a conflict between them. Even her "sub-goddesses" are fearsome: Badbh the battle crow, Nemain the inciter of frenzy, and Macha, with regard to whom it was said that heads severed in battle were "Macha's Acorn Crop" (see Chapter 9 for more on this important goddess).

Although the old tales do give evidence that the Morrigán was not afraid to get her hands bloody, she was not so much a killing machine herself as an ally of those who did "the dirty work." She supported her warriors as an inspirer of fear. In other words, the magic she conjured on a battlefield would not so much directly kill the foes of her devotees as simply smite them with a nameless dread. She particularly aimed her terror at those whose hearts were already faltering, pursuing the fleeing enemies so that their panic and confusion would only increase with every retreating step. A brilliant strategy, for what could bring down an army faster than to have its own members pummeling headlong into one another, not knowing where safety lies and becoming fodder for each other's paranoia?

And yet, the Phantom Queen knew firsthand the taste of the kill. One especially grisly tale recounts how, to whip the warriors of the Túatha Dé Danann into a battle frenzy, she slaughtered one of their enemies, Indech the Fomorian, and filled her hands with his blood—which she then dispersed among her own heroes. A baptism of blood, not for the fainthearted. But then, nothing that the Morrigán touches or transforms is gentle or kind. She is rough, edgy, and dangerous; she dwells in those places where adrenaline flows vigorously and the heart pounds relentlessly, whether from four-alarm anxiety or the thrill of killing or the primal passion of hard, raw sex.

Like many Celtic deities, the Morrigán was an accomplished magician, specializing in the above-mentioned shapeshifting and fearmongering.

These qualities speak of her as a guardian of altered states of consciousness. In the modern world, she would be the goddess of bad LSD trips or of nervous breakdowns. Her terrain would cover all psychotic episodes, from the shattering withdrawal of catatonic schizophrenia to the cool and methodical designs of a patient serial killer.

Lady of the Summer's End

Naturally, the time of year most sacred to this terrible figure can only be Samhain—the festival of death. The tradition upholds this, for one of the most powerful stories of Irish lore, in which the Phantom Queen enjoys a passionate tryst with the Dagda while standing astride the Unshin River in County Sligo, is set on this sacred day. It makes perfect sense, for both the Morrigán and the Dagda (see Chapter 14) represent a nexus of the energies of death as well as life. Consider: When she's not rallying her favored warriors to kill (or discarding them to be killed), she's perfectly willing to embrace the primal power of sex—in other words, her innate feminine power as a giver of life. In a similar way, the Dagda rules both of these energies, for his club can either kill (nine foes with a single blow) or, at its opposite end, restore life to those who have fallen. He's a powerful warrior, and yet his cauldron issues forth abundance beyond measure. Death and life—embraced within both of these deities.

So this goddess of fear cannot be divorced from the erotic force she embodies in her union with the Dagda. Their union, the sacred marriage of death and life, marks the energies of Samhain, the festival of summer's end. Many Neo-Pagans see Samhain strictly as a time of honoring the dead, while Beltaine is the sexier holiday of maypole dances and all-night orgies. Celtic wisdom, however, reminds us that the union of the energies of life and death is closer than most of us would care to admit. Hence, the goddess of war couples with the god of abundance at the threshold between the light and dark halves of the year. Significantly, after satisfying her body's hunger with the Dagda, she begins to prophesy, foretelling the battle that will enable the Túatha Dé Danann to win Ireland from the oppressive hand of the Fomorians. Out of the union of death and life comes renewal, expressed through her words of knowledge and foresight from the spiritual realm.

Approaching the Phantom Queen

So why would any sane person invoke the Morrigán today? What good can possibly come out of dealing with a goddess so frightful, treacherous, and dangerous? To answer this question, we need to consider the uncomfortable truth that, like it or not, the Morrigán resides within each one of us. John Lennon once said, "We are all Christ and we're all Hitler." In other words, don't just look for the cozy, sweet love of a nurturing goddess like Brigit within you; just a heartbeat or a brainwave away from her gentle flame, you will find the ravaging fires of a powerful killer queen. We must learn to deal with the Morrigán, because if we do not keep an eye on her (or on her energies within us), then we run the risk of a surprise attack. And that, in our overcrowded and stressed-out world, is not something any of us can afford. Rather than ignore the goddess of war until she inspires us to explode (whether at a loved one, on the highway, or in any other setting), far better to pay her the respect she deserves all along—which includes training the warrior spirit within yourself to the point where you can move through life with the graceful power and confidence of one who fears no person or thing.

Of course, the Morrigán demands our attention for reasons beyond simply trying to contain her havoc. The close connection between the Washer at the Ford and the lusty lover means there is always a bit of Beltaine in every Samhain (and vice versa). This, indeed, is a glimpse into the deeper mysteries of the Celtic tradition.

Because the Morrigán is so scary and dark, not nearly as much of her wisdom and lore has survived, especially when compared to the available lore relating to a "nicer" figure like Brigit. The Morrigán refused to be taken prisoner by the coming of Christianity and the monotheistic society it represented. She was last seen howling and shrieking at the Battle of Clontarf in 1017. Perhaps this in itself is a miracle—that the Phantom Queen could still appear five centuries after Ireland first encountered the new religion! But whereas Brigit submitted to the constricting yoke of the nun's habit, the Morrigán chose to retreat into the darkness of the underworld (her legendary haunt is a cave in the west of Ireland at Rath Cruachain, traditionally the seat of the kings and queens of Connacht), where she could bide her time.

And perhaps, now, her time has come. She returned to the Irish consciousness in the form of a raven perched on the shoulder of the dying Cú Chulainn, part of a moving statue in Dublin that commemorates the fallen heroes of the rebellion in 1916. This rebellion sparked the war for Irish independence, which resulted in the formation in 1921 of the first sovereign Celtic nation in hundreds of years. More recently, the Morrigán has become one of the most popular goddesses among feminists and Neo-Pagans, many of whom are drawn to her take-no-prisoners personality.

How do we honor the Morrigán today? Perhaps more than with any other Celtic deity, working with the Phantom Queen is no task for beginners. She does not tolerate fear; indeed, if she smells it on you she will probably just make it worse. Better to confine your initial spiritual work with less-threatening deities such as Lugh or Brigit. But if you can find the courage in your heart to face down your own fears and to own (and transform) your own capacity for murderous rage or your potential to grind out your sexual appetites with no thought of love or tenderness, then you may be ready to call the Morrigán's energies into your life. Some ways to do this can include mastering a martial art, exercising to achieve and maintain peak physical fitness, participating in therapy to face and heal your fears (or other threatening emotions), serving (or supporting those who serve) in the armed forces, and meditating on your own mortality (which, in itself, is advanced magical work, and should only be done with the support of a spiritual teacher and/or counselor).

If you have an established relationship with a sexual partner, sex magic can be particularly powerful when dedicated to the Phantom Queen—but once again, this is not for beginners. More than one couple has discovered that invoking the Morrigán and the Dagda in a Neo-Pagan Samhain ritual can lead to such a mutual sexual charge (even among those who have been married for years) that, without proper grounding, it can lead to night after night of rapturous sex—which interferes with work and every other aspect of life! For this reason, it is not wise to invoke the Morrigán's energy in the context of a new intimate or sexual relationship. As a goddess who expressed wrath when she was sexually rejected, she is not the deity to call on for navigating the difficult waters of starting a romance.

Remember, the Morrigán is powerful; therefore, she not only respects power, but demands that her devotees embody their own maximum power. If she scares you, don't work with her. She'll respect you if you say, "Not yet."

Chapter 8

Medb:
She Who Intoxicates

One of the most colorful and striking figures in the Irish tradition appears as a scheming, manipulative harridan, who is almost single-handedly responsible for what is perhaps the most tragic event in Irish mythology, the great cattle raid of Cooley. As she is portrayed in the stories recorded in the Middle Ages, Queen Medb of Connacht doesn't come off well. She is vindictive, aggressive, promiscuous, coldhearted, ruthless, and willing to expend the lives of numerous warriors before sacrificing the smallest bit of pride before her royal husband.

Indeed, this warrior queen is portrayed so unsympathetically, any discerning reader might wonder, *Why?* What motivated the scribes who first committed her story to vellum to depict her as such a wanton mistress of death and mayhem? Indeed, this question may be the single most important gateway into the mysteries of this hidden goddess. For beneath the capricious, overly aggressive queen, an older and more appealing figure begins to take shape—not a queen, but a goddess who may well have been the most sublime personification of sovereignty (the freedom of the land and the source of the king's right to rule) in the history of Ireland.

The first clue to understanding Medb involves understanding her name. Like Brigit or the Morrigán, she is a figure whose name is actually a title— Medb means "she who intoxicates." It's a name etymologically linked to another word that will be familiar to modern readers with an interest in alcoholic beverages: *mead*. Indeed, a variant spelling of her name is Mcadhbh. This in itself may not mean so much—after all, Medb is quite a sexy figure, and wouldn't it make sense for a queen with an insatiable appetite for men to be an intoxicating woman? But her link to fermented honey long predates her role as a warmonger, for in many Indo-European cultures, rituals of inauguration for kings included the ceremonial sharing of a sacred beverage between a priestess (who represented the goddess) and the new ruler. In Ireland, such rituals were called *banais righe*, or "the wedding-feast of kingship," and included sexual union between the king and the representative of the goddess, and his receiving a libation from her. The beverage typically used in such rituals was wine—or mead.

Indeed, the inauguration ceremonies indicate that the king's ability to rule is bestowed upon him by the goddess/priestess; the sharing of the mead functions as a symbolic marriage between the king (as representative of the human community) and the goddess (who personifies the land). The land goddess herself is Sovereignty—the personification of freedom and the authority to rule. Many mythic tales depict the close relationship between the king and this goddess; one well-known legend concerns a fourth-century Irish king, Niall of the Nine Hostages. As a young man, he encounters a goddess in the form of an old hag guarding a well. When the youth agrees to mate with the crone in exchange for water, he is rewarded with a vision of her in her divine glory. She declares that she is Sovereignty, and because he has accepted her, she likewise accepts him as the one worthy to be high king.

The Divine Wife of Kings

As Sovereignty, the goddess is the source of a king's authority and power. Just as Christian rulers in later ages declared that a king ruled by divine right granted to him from God, so the Pagan Celts understood that authority came from a sacred source—from the land herself, in her sovereign aspect. The tradition also makes it clear that a just and worthy king would reign over a land filled with abundance and prosperity, but that the goddess would turn against a bad or unfit king, causing crop failure and other maladies that would proclaim his unworthiness as a ruler. As with any other relationship, for it to prosper, both parties (king/society and goddess/land) had to benefit from the union.

Tradition holds that before she became queen of Connacht (the western province of Ireland), Medb's home was Tara. Because the Hill of Tara had long been associated with the high king and the authority over all of Ireland, this association testifies to Medb's original function as personification of sovereignty—perhaps *the* goddess of Sovereignty, equal to other primary deities like Brigit or Danu. Befitting her role, it was said that Medb would not permit a man to be king over Ireland unless he first took her as his wife. In other words, the land would not support the authority of a king who had not pledged to be the land's "lover."

The tradition suggests that Medb was married to nine kings. This is not a jab at her for being some sort of primeval polyamorist—rather it speaks to her role as a goddess. For kings come and go, but the land is forever renewed by the cleansing cycle of the seasons. Medb's unending cycle of enjoying the pleasures of a new lover simply acknowledges Sovereignty's function as the perpetual bride who offers her mead cup again and again to each successive king.

The Worst Possible Depiction

With this background in mind, suddenly the behavior of the wicked queen who drives the action of the great Irish epic *Táin Bó Cuailnge* ("The Cattle Raid of Cooley") begins to make perfect sense. The *Táin* begins with Medb engaged in a lover's conversation with her husband, King Ailill of Connacht. She praises him for his generosity, kindness, courage, and lack of jealousy with these famous lines: "If I married a jealous man that would be wrong, too: I never had one man without another waiting in his shadow." (*The Tain*, trans. Thomas Kinsella, p. 53). These are not the words of a nymphomaniac, but rather the reasonable observation of Lady Sovereignty.

Medb's identity as Sovereignty is, however, hidden by her guise as a cattle-raiding queen. She gleefully declares how she loves to stir up trouble, and she insists that she, not Ailill, is the head of their household. When he challenges that claim, she demands they take inventory to see which of them is the possessor of the greater fortune (for that, not gender, would determine the head of their house). When she discovers that she lacks a magnificent bull to match one that belongs to Ailill, she sets out to acquire one—setting in motion a series of unfortunate events that will culminate in tremendous bloodshed, her own humiliation, and the unrelenting violence of Ireland's greatest hero, Cú Chulainn.

The *Táin* features the worst possible depiction of Medb, and yet it has become the most famous tale in which she figures. Aside from her petty scheming, it's a tale in which Cú Chulainn makes fun of her, taunts her for being a woman, and shows her up in terms of his skill. When she tries to trick him, he sees through her maneuverings. Her greatest humiliation is depicted when he stumbles across her during her menstrual time. Clearly in a vulnerable position, she pleads with him to spare her life; he agrees, but not without expressing his scorn—he tells the queen he is "not a killer of women." Given his contempt, is it surprising Medb eventually conspires to have Cú Chulainn killed?

But the champion of Ulster is not the only man whose doom is arranged by the intoxicating queen. In other stories, Medb has lovers killed—including her husband Ailill, who finally gets jealous and himself slays one of her favorite boy toys. Eventually Medb dies violently, according to one tale, by her nephew. Medb had killed one of her sisters while the woman was pregnant, and the baby was ripped from his dying mother's womb. Years later, the boy sees Medb bathing in the water and asks who the woman is. When he is told that this is his mother's sister and murderer, he throws the handiest object—as it turns out, a piece of hard cheese—striking her mortally.

So we are left with this tantalizing question: How did an awesome goddess of sovereignty get reduced to the role of a petty regional queen, whose intrigues result in all sorts of bloodshed?

Some scholars have speculated that many of the more colorful depictions of Medb, involving her numerous lovers and the jealousy and drama that ensue, are largely literary inventions of the Middle Ages, without any real basis in the ancient myths. Even if it really were the unashamed eroticism as Medb-as-Sovereignty that led to her reinvention as the paragon of Celtic promiscuity, the manner in which her sexual escapades are presented speak far more of appalled Christian piety than of ancient Pagan mystery. It's almost as if the men who wrote about Medb in medieval times needed to "sex her up," both as a way of attempting to tame such a strong feminine character and because it made for a more entertaining story!

One way to understand Medb could be to consider her in light of the Pagan Irish goddess who most successfully reinvented herself within the Christian faith: Brigit, who inspired (or became) the great Christian saint who bears her name. In many ways, Medb is Brigit's alter ego. Originally a goddess of agriculture and the sacred land, Brigit survived after the coming of Christianity in the form of a pious virgin saint. Medb, however, did not fare so well: she was transformed into a wanton, promiscuous schemer. Brigit attained a new, if somewhat docile, role as a model of feminine spiritual authority under the new religious order, but Medb, whose very name means "intoxication" and whose primary role was to offer authority and power to men through her mead and her thighs, could find no place within the structures of the new religion. Like the fearsome Morrigán, she is in essence an untamable goddess. Thus, the tradition transformed Medb into a power-hungry virago, a woman who today symbolizes addiction instead of the grace and bounty of the earth. Celtic tradition is the poorer because of this.

Restoring Medb

It is now time to restore Medb to her authentic place as a goddess, reaching into the deepest recesses of her past to find the divine figure who is powerful without being manipulative; sovereign without being hostile; and erotic with joy and exuberance, not with a veiled aggression that could be written off as mere immorality.

What are we to make of Medb? How can we assist her in the revival of her function as a goddess? Perhaps the best way to approach her is through her most controversial quality: her sexuality. People who embrace alternative or controversial expressions of sexuality (from gay, lesbian, and bisexual sexuality to polyamory and BDSM) could venerate Medb, the goddess of exuberant eroticism who was misunderstood and vilified for her sexuality. Indeed, Medb could be invoked for healing and assistance in any situation in which someone has been unfairly maligned or rejected for moral reasons. She is a goddess who particularly adores strong, vivacious, sexually confident women, and who also looks kindly upon men who are courageous, generous, kind-hearted, and confident rather than jealous. Of course, she also has a particular affection for men who are in positions of authority—or who are just plain gorgeous!

Venerate Medb today by cultivating your confidence and ambition. Honor Medb by going after—and attaining—the finer things in life. Don't expect her to bless you for being timid or shy, but rather call on her to bestow her favor on your efforts to make dreams come true (even if they're dreams that carry a bit of controversy). Finally, consider Medb as a symbol of addiction—if you are struggling with letting go of an addiction, or bringing balance into your life, Medb is probably not the best goddess to work with. Turn to Brigit or Rhiannon instead.

Because of her exuberant sexuality, Medb is best honored at the two festivals most strongly linked with sex: Beltaine and Samhain. And it might also make sense to pour a libation of mead or wine to her whenever a president is inaugurated, a king crowned, or any other head of state formally installed.

Chapter 9

Macha:
Goddess of Many Lives

1

The mythic origin of Irish history is recounted in a book called *Lebor Gabála Érenn* ("The Book of the Taking of Ireland"), which details a series of legendary invasions in which succeeding tribes or communities of people and/or gods came to live in the Emerald Isle. Five different groups of settlers preceded the arrival of the Celts, who have remained the primary residents of the land to this very day. According to the myth, the third invasion was led by a hero named Nemed and his wife, Macha. Nemed's tribe, the Nemedians, set about clearing pastureland in Ireland for their settlement; one of those pastures was named for Macha, and eventually became her resting place when she died. Her death came about because of a broken heart—for she was a prophetess, and prophesied the tragedies what would ensue because of the great cattle raid of Cooley. Her burial place became known as Macha's Height, in Irish *Ard Macha*—the original name of the city now called Armagh. As Nemed's wife, the Lady Macha is a goddess of fertility and sovereignty, linked with the land (especially, but not only, the land that bears her name).

II

In the days of Conchobar mac Nessa, the great king of Ulster, a farmer named Crunniuc experienced what could only be termed the ultimate single man's fantasy. Recently widowed, the farmer was quite wealthy, but lonely. One day, however, a lovely Otherworldly woman simply arrived at his house, and began tending to the domestic chores. Surprised and a bit amazed, Crunniuc noticed her performing a ritualized movement, turning sunwise before entering the house and before climbing into bed with him and offering her love. Entranced by the fairy maiden's beauty, industry, and strength, the farmer could only wonder at his good fortune. He learned that his new love was named Macha, and she asked only one thing of him: that he tell no one about her.

All seemed to go well. Crunniuc's farm prospered more than ever, and soon Macha's body began to swell with their child. The time came for the great assembly of the Ulstermen; as the farmer prepared to go, Macha reminded him of his promise not to mention her. But she underestimated the weakness of his character. Upon watching a chariot race where the king's finest horses won handily, Crunniuc boasted that his wife could outrun any of the horses at the assembly. In a horse culture like that of the ancient Celts, these were fighting words—and soon the hapless farmer found himself in prison, the angry king warning him that if he didn't prove his claim, his life would be forfeit.

Messengers brought the heavily pregnant Macha before the king. Horrified at this turn of events, she begged for mercy—after all, her time for birth was fast approaching. But the king was blinded by the perceived insult and demanded that she race against his horses or her husband would die. Because her honor was greater than her husband's ability to keep a secret, she agreed. As she raced—easily outstripping even the fastest horse—she cried out that she was Macha, daughter of Sainrith mac Imbaith—which means "strange son of the ocean"—and that a terrible curse would fall on the men of Ulster because of their lack of compassion. She was the first to cross the finish line, thereby saving her husband's life and honor. But as she did so, she screamed in terrible pain and gave birth to twins—which, combined with the stress of the race, cost her life. In her dying throes, Macha uttered the terms of the curse: The men of Ulster would, at their hour of greatest need, be struck with debilitating pain that mimicked the pains of childbirth. It would last for five days and four nights, and would afflict the Ulstermen for nine times nine generations.

And with that, the Otherworldly Macha, of the speed greater than horses, mother of the twins, died.

III

In the fourth century B.C.E., a great queen known as Macha Mong Ruadh—"Macha of the Red Hair"—lived in Ulster. Her story is one of intrigue and fierce combat, as she had to defeat several rivals (according to some versions of the story, her two main rivals were her uncles) before she could command the throne. Eventually, she married Cimbáeth, one of her chief rivals, and promptly overpowered his sons, whom she then commanded to build a great fortress, the dimensions of which were drawn by a clasp she wore about her neck. This fortress was named Emhain Macha, or the "Jewel of Macha." Among her other achievements, this Queen Macha is credited with opening Ireland's first hospital, which existed for several centuries, until it was burned in the year 22 of the Common Era.

Goddess of the Three Functions

Clearly, Macha—or a series of heroines and goddesses bearing this name—is one of the most frequently recurring figures in Irish lore. In addition to the previous stories, she was married to Nuadu of the Silver Hand, one of the great kings of the Túatha Dé Danann. Macha is perhaps best known as a war goddess—called "the battle crow," one of the three dark sisters who are aspects of the Morrigán in her plural form as the Mórrígna (the Phantom Queens). As mentioned in Chapter 7, one of the more macabre images associated with Macha is that of severed heads lying on a battlefield—carnage that was called Macha's Acorn Crop.

Are these all different goddesses, or perhaps the same powerful figure appearing in different forms at different times? This is the great mystery of Macha. She embodies the spirit of Sovereignty, associated with pastureland, and later with horses; but she is also a prophetess, capable of receiving visions so terrifying that they could kill her; and she is a warrior, a fearless queen, capable of subduing multiple rivals and striking terror into the hearts of men thanks to her stomach-wrenching battle crop.

Scholars have long suggested that ancient Celtic society, like most other Indo-European cultures, could be divided roughly into three categories:

1. Farmers and producers.
2. Priests and priestesses and other wisdom keepers.
3. Warriors and nobility.

When Julius Caesar described the Celts in his book *The Gallic War*, he commented that their two leading classes were the knights and the druids—the warriors and the wisdom keepers, respectively.

What makes Macha so fascinating is how she embodies each of these three functions. In her earliest incarnation, she is both the prophetess (the wisdom function) and the goddess of Sovereignty (the farming function). She returns as the wife of Crunniuc in her Sovereignty function, but in an inverted way—instead of marrying the king, she marries a farmer and, in fact, is indirectly killed by the king. This violation of the natural order requires punishment, and so, as she dies, Macha utters her famous curse on the men of Ulster. Finally, Macha of the Red Hair seems to be the least "divine" of the mythic Macha's, but stands alongside her namesakes as the embodiment of the warrior function—apparently doing it so well that she becomes ever after associated with battle and its fearsome consequences.

Macha's "Home"

Throughout the Celtic world, goddesses are associated with place. Examples that we've seen include Brigit, associated with Kildare; Boann, associated with the Boyne River and the Boyne Valley; Medb, associated with the Hill of Tara and with Rath Crúachain in County Roscommon; Anu, associated with two hills called the Two Paps of Anu at the County Cork–County Kerry border. There are numerous others. Macha, of course, will forever be associated with Emhain Macha in Ulster, a ritual site that in terms of mythology is regarded as the seat of the Ulster kings, meaning it has associations not only with Macha, but with Cú Chulainn, Conchobar, and many other significant heroes of myth.

Today, Emhain Macha is little more than a beautiful hill to the west of Armagh, its ritual origins now only faintly discernible in the highly eroded earthworks that surround the summit. But, once upon a time, a great temple had been built there, only to be ritually set on fire—perhaps a massive sacrifice to the gods at a time of great need. So little is known about Emhain Macha that scholars cannot even reach consensus on the meaning of its name; indeed, the myths offer conflicting ideas as to its origin. The mysterious word *Emhain* could mean "jewel," but it could also mean "twins." The tale of Crunniuc's Otherworldly lover culminates in her giving birth to twins, implying that Emhain Macha was named for her children; but as we've seen, the story of Macha Mong Ruadh suggests that it was for a jewel clasped around the queen's neck that this ancient site was named. Like so much else in our incomplete record of Celtic lore, this must finally remain a mystery.

Honoring Macha

Thanks to her multifaceted and complex character, today we can honor Macha in a variety of ways. In her we see war, fertility, abundance, prophecy, and sovereignty. These are the great characteristics of Irish goddesses throughout the tradition. Use your imagination, and it's easy to begin to make connections between these mighty themes: The land is the source of both sovereignty and fertility, and it is in the service of sovereignty that sometimes the spirit of the warrior must be invoked. The horse is a symbol of all these qualities: Warriors ride horses, but farmers plow with them; so the horse joins battle and fertility together. As for prophecy, it represents that third function that holds the other two together: wisdom, the key to balancing the sometimes conflicting needs of the producers and the nobility.

Obviously, Macha can stand alongside Epona and Rhiannon (see Chapter 10) as a goddess venerated through all things equine. But it is a mistake to see her as a cognate of her Welsh and Gaulish cousins. Her battle function links her with the Morrigán; her sovereignty function means she is similar to Medb and Anu; and her prophetic function places her alongside Brigit and the Morrigán again. Thus, one way to venerate Macha would be through efforts to honor the entire sweep of your life: your work, your home, your spirituality, and your family. Depending on your career, your work could require either the "warrior" energy or the "producer" energy (and sometimes both). The home, meanwhile, is certainly the abode of Lady Sovereignty—for a "man's home is his castle" (and the same goes for a woman!). So one way to honor Macha would be through efforts to improve the quality of your life in holistic ways. Given the particulars of her story, she is also very much a patroness of athletic skill (particularly track and field), housecleaning, motherhood, leadership (particularly women in authority), hospitals, and divination.

One final note: The great hero Cú Chulainn has a horse called the Gray of Macha—perhaps because this horse was as fast as the goddess!

Chapter 10

Rhiannon:
The Great Queen

hiannon is one of the best-loved goddesses of the Welsh pantheon; thanks to a hit song by the 70s rock group Fleetwood Mac, even many non-Celts know her name. Part of Rhiannon's popularity comes from the fullness of her mythology. We can actually construct a nearly complete tale of her life and activities, a rather rare occurrence in the world of Celtic deities.

Rhiannon's story reads almost like a fairy tale—not so surprising when we realize that it was written down during the High Middle Ages, when romantic stories of chivalry and the supernatural were extremely popular. As in most Welsh mythology, medieval (and Christian) elements creep into the telling of the old tale. It is as if the characters are traveling incognito, but their updated manners and garments cannot conceal their true identity as ancient beings of more-than-human greatness.

We meet Rhiannon in the First Branch of the Mabinogi. One day during a feast, Pwyll, ruler of Dyfed in southern Wales, decides to climb the mysterious Mound of Arberth. Any noble who sits atop this mound is fated either to suffer an injury or to see a marvel, and soon Pwyll beholds a vision indeed: a beautiful woman, richly clad, riding slowly past on a white mare. He must know who she is, and sends one rider after another to find out. Yet however fast his messengers ride, they cannot catch up to the lady, even though her horse appears to be walking at a slow, even pace. At last, Pwyll himself rides after the mysterious woman, driving his horse to exhaustion without coming near to reaching her. In desperation he calls out,

"Lady, for the sake of the one you love best, I beg you to stop!" She halts immediately, turns to Pwyll, and tells him, "It would have been better for your horse if you had asked me to stop sooner."

In spite of this rebuke, Rhiannon has come to Arberth specifically to seek Pwyll as her husband. After a few misadventures, they are finally wed. They do not live quite happily ever after, however. Although they remain loving and faithful to each other, more trials await them. The worst is the abduction of their newborn son during the night after his birth. Rhiannon's waiting women, who fell asleep when they were supposed to be on watch, accuse their mistress of having killed the baby, and the nobles of Pwyll's court demand she be punished. Her penalty is to wait at the horseblock by the fortress gate and offer to carry visitors to the court on her back; she is sentenced to do this every day for seven years. But in the fourth year, a nobleman named Teyrnon Twrf Liant arrives with his foster son, Gwri Goldenhair, whom he had found as a newborn that mysteriously appeared at his door—just after his favorite mare had borne a colt on May Eve. After hearing how Rhiannon lost her own child, Teyrnon realizes that Gwri is the missing heir of Dyfed. With her child restored to her, Rhiannon exclaims, "Now I am delivered of my anxiety (*pryder*)," and her son is known as Pryderi thereafter.

This is where the First Branch ends, but it is not the conclusion of Rhiannon's story. We encounter her again in the Third Branch. At this point Pwyll is dead, and Pryderi is a grown man who has succeeded to the lordship of Dyfed. Returning from a disastrous war in Ireland, Pryderi brings home his friend Manawydan with the idea that he might marry Rhiannon. So it happens, and this marriage too is a happy one, although again not without its troubles.

When Pryderi disappears into an enchanted fortress, Rhiannon goes after him and likewise disappears. Through a combination of patience, luck, and cleverness, Manawydan wins their release from the enchantment. He learns, moreover, that during Rhiannon's imprisonment in the fortress, she was forced to endure the punishment of wearing around her neck the collars of donkeys that had been hauling hay.

Rhiannon also figures indirectly in the Second Branch of the Mabinogi. Toward the end of this story, the weary survivors of the war in Ireland spend seven years in a feast hall, where the three birds of Rhiannon sing to them: "and all the songs they had ever heard were coarse compared to that one." The birds of Rhiannon are mentioned again in the early Welsh

Arthurian tale "Culhwch and Olwen," where we learn that their song has the power to wake the dead and give rest to the living.

Horses, Sovereignty, and the Otherworld

The surviving myths tell us several things about Rhiannon. Most clearly, she has a strong connection with horses and other equines. Horses played an important role in early Celtic society. They were admired for their beauty, strength, speed, fertility, and sexual potency. They not only performed humble farm tasks, but also carried aristocratic warriors into battle, either on their backs or in wickerwork chariots. So the horse was a helper, a bearer of burdens, a means of transport, as well as a symbol and enabler of strength, prowess, and nobility. Fighting on horseback or from a chariot was a prerogative of the elite, a partnership of noble warrior and horse.

Horses figured in the symbology of another and similar partnership, that between king and land, or king and sovereignty. For example, the medieval churchman Giraldus Cambrensis recorded (and perhaps sensationalized) an Irish kingship rite in which a white mare stood for sovereignty, to which the king was symbolically mated. (Such a ceremony may have been related to the inauguration rituals associated with Medb. See Chapter 8.) The idea beneath seems to be, at least in part, that the goddess of sovereignty must literally carry the ruler. He does not control her; if he treats her ill, she may throw him from her back. Only through a proper partnership can the realm flourish.

Another expression of this concept is found in the Second Branch, when a brother of the British king mutilates horses belonging to the Irish king—not only a cruel act but an extremely insulting one that sets the stage for the terrible war between Ireland and Britain. The horses here are connected with Branwen, who is counted as one of the three ancestresses or great queens of Britain. Sister of the British king, wife of the Irish king, her marriage was intended to bring the two realms together. But because of the mutilation of the horses, her husband strikes her and banishes her to his kitchens.[1] Her brothers come to her rescue, and the war ensues—with the result that both lands are laid waste, and Branwen dies, returning to the earth.

The horse's importance, in daily life and religion alike, seems to have been nearly universal among the Celts. One evidence of this was the artistic skill that was lavished on horse trappings, which provide some of the finest examples of Celtic metalworking, even in the distant Celtic kingdom of Galatia, in what is now central Turkey. Archaeology has also turned up widespread instances of burials of horses. In some cases, these were probably animals given honorable treatment after their death from warfare or other causes. It is also clear that numerous horse burials contain the bodies of sacrificed animals—and the Celts typically sacrificed things that they valued highly. In the case of horses, the value was so great that some scholars conclude these sacrifices were made only for the greatest of needs.

Goddesses connected with horses are known from both British and Irish mythology and, from an even earlier period, Gaulish statues and inscriptions. The Gaulish horse goddess was named Epona; her very name comes from the Gaulish word for "horse," *epos.* She gained a special popularity because Roman cavalry officers—many of them originally from Gaul—adopted her as their patroness and carried her worship all over the Roman Empire.

Numerous Romano-Celtic statues and reliefs of Epona have been discovered. She is always depicted with horses. Some images show her riding a mare sidesaddle (an interesting contrast to Celtic coins that depict women riding astride), often accompanied by a foal. Sometimes the mare is nursing the foal, while in other cases Epona is feeding the foal from a *patera,* or shallow offering bowl. Other images show the goddess standing or seated between two horses or two groups of horses. The other important aspect of these depictions of Epona is that she is often holding a bag, cornucopia, fruit, grain, or bread. Occasionally she is portrayed with a key or a napkin.

This imagery of Epona, along with written evidence from the Roman world, shows that she was worshipped as a goddess of abundance and fertility as well as of horses, horse breeding, riders, and stables. The fruit and grain also connect her with the earth and its fertility. But what about the key and the napkin? Some scholars interpret the key in light of Epona's protection of stables—she locks the stable doors against harm, for example. Another interpretation is that the key she holds is that which unlocks the joys of the Otherworld. The napkin also has both a worldly and religious explanation: It is the napkin that a Roman official would drop to signal the start of a horse or chariot race; but that race could symbolize the course of a person's life. Epona's napkin might indicate that she plays a role in the beginning of each person's life journey, just as the key could symbolize her role at the end of life. This is supported by the fact that, in her images, she is often accompanied by a dog, which could symbolize both healing and death in the Romano-Celtic world.

Interestingly, Rhiannon's first husband, Pwyll, has a close relationship with dogs at the beginning of the First Branch. But Rhiannon connects with Epona in even stronger ways, starting with the role horses play for both goddesses. Then there is the aspect of abundance: Rhiannon becomes noted for her generosity when she distributes lavish gifts to the nobles of Dyfed after her marriage to Pwyll. At her wedding feast, she also reveals that she owns a magical bag that can hold an infinite amount of food. In the Third Branch, her disappearance is part of a pattern of magical disruption in Dyfed, which suffers the loss of its people, livestock, and crops; when Rhiannon returns, so does the abundance of the land.

Rhiannon seems clearly to be a goddess of the earth and the Otherworld. The place where she comes from is never specified in the Mabinogi, but it is easy to conclude that she has entered Dyfed from the Mound of Arberth itself. Landmarks such as this—which were often pre-Celtic burial mounds—were widely regarded by the Celts as entrances to the Otherworld, or places from which the Otherworld could impinge on this world. Rhiannon's first marriage also affirms her Otherworldly aspect. When she seeks Pwyll, she is actually betrothed to a lord named Gwawl, whose name means "light." In contrast, Pwyll is a man who has not only visited the Otherworld and made an alliance with its ruler, but has even been granted the title Pen Annwn, "Chief of the Otherworld" (literally "Head of the Deep"). It is not the lord of light, but the lord of the Otherworld whom Rhiannon loves. Together, she and Pwyll form a link between the worlds, for the benefit of the people of Dyfed.

There are so many parallels between Rhiannon and Epona that most people tend to think of Rhiannon as a later British version of the Gaulish goddess. And for all we know, Rhiannon's "real name" may have been Epona; *Rhiannon* is simply a title, most often interpreted to mean "Great Queen." (And, in fact, a Roman epithet for Epona was *Regina*, "Queen.") This reminds us that, along with all her other areas of concern, she is an embodiment of Sovereignty. In recent years, John Matthews has coined a new title for Rhiannon, which we quite like: "The Lady of the Sacred Earth."

Rhiannon at the Holy Days

In the First Branch of the Mabinogi, Rhiannon's newborn son is found by Teyrnon Twrf Liant on May Eve (April 30), the night on which his remarkable mare gives birth to a colt every year. The connection between

Rhiannon's motherhood, a mare, and this particular point in the Wheel of the Year is so strong that we can regard this in many ways as Rhiannon's own holiday.

April 30–May 1 is one of the major Celtic (and, today, Wiccan and Neo-Pagan) festivals. In medieval Wales, May Day was known as Cyntefin, "The First of Summer;" in modern Welsh it is Calan Mai, "The First Day of May." It stands at the opposite point of the year from Calan Gaeaf, "The First Day of Winter"—Samhain, or Halloween. These two holidays mark the boundaries between the light and dark halves of the year, summer and winter. Both are times when the veil between this world and the Otherworld is said to be at its thinnest.

On the nights when the veil is thin, humans can be open to possibilities, but also vulnerable to perils. May Eve has, therefore, traditionally been a time for bonfires, vigils, and (because Otherworld knowledge may be more available), divination. In the First Branch, Teyrnon Twrf Liant spent May Eve keeping vigil over his mare to make sure that her colt would not be stolen away as it had been in previous years. A strong, sturdy colt was born soon after dark and stood almost immediately. Then a great claw reached through the window and snatched at its mane. Teyrnon cut away the arm, but although he ran outside to chase after the monster, he saw nothing more of it. This mysterious monster typifies the uncertainties of life, the unseen and unexpected dangers that are always lurking behind our illusions of security. At the same time, however, the story teaches us that one who stays awake and alert may not only defeat such threats, but also receive great and unlooked-for gifts.

After the "night of madness," as May Eve is sometimes called, the morning brings the joys of the new-begun summer, with its promises of abundance. In the British Isles (and places with similar climate) the life force is waxing strong at Calan Mai. May Day customs from the Middle Ages and the early modern era included decorating homes with greenery and flowers; in Wales birch branches were often the decoration of choice. Celebrations emphasized music, dancing, game playing, and courting. Folklorist Trefor M. Owen has written that in parts of Wales, "May Day generally saw the beginning of a summer season of open-air activities, including those associated with the *twmpath chwarae* (lit. 'play mound')…. On the mound would be seated the harper or fiddler who would be employed for the season to accompany the dancing which would be the main pastime during the long summer evenings…. Games were also played, including tennis and bowling, throwing the stone and beam, and wrestling…."

This life-affirming holiday seems the perfect time for telling the story of how Rhiannon rode out of the Otherworld to claim the man she loved—and to join with him to ensure that both land and people would flourish.

Rhiannon also has a connection with the harvest season, when her husband Manawydan's efforts to harvest his grain fields bring about her return from her imprisonment in the enchanted fortress. A case can be made for honoring Rhiannon during Yuletide, too: In the imperial Roman calendar, December 18 was the feast day of Epona. Moreover, images of the divine mother and child (in a stable, no less!) are so prevalent at this time of year that it can be an apt time for paying homage to Rhiannon in her aspect as mother.

The south Welsh Christmas-season tradition of the Mari Lwyd ("Gray Mare") may possibly be a distant echo of ancient observances or may be a manifestation of a similar current of belief. Even if the timing is just a coincidence, the Mari Lwyd is certainly of interest in relation to Rhiannon/Epona. The Mari Lwyd was, again in the words of Trefor M. Owen, "a horse's skull covered with a white sheet and decorated with colourful ribbons; this was carried by a man concealed under the sheet who could operate the jaw and make it snap." Accompanied by a group of men, the Mari Lwyd was taken from door to door throughout a village or neighborhood: "The party, normally dressed up as Sergeant, Merryman, Punch and Judy, led the *Mari* to the door of the house and engaged in a poetic contest, often singing as many as fifteen verses before they were eventually allowed to enter. The *Mari,* on entering the house, would run wildly after the girls snapping at them with its jaws until the time came to enjoy the food and drink offered in plenty."

Every Day with Rhiannon

Perhaps the most concrete way to connect with Rhiannon is through horses, although this may not be an option for many people. But getting to know horses better is a way of knowing this goddess better—even if the closest approach open to some of us is through books or movies such as *Seabiscuit* and *The Black Stallion.* If we are serving food in honor of Rhiannon, oatcakes, oatmeal cookies, or even oat porridge can also help us touch that equine aspect. And horses are not the only animals related to Rhiannon—songbirds, too, are sacred to her. So feeding the birds—in the backyard, on the fire escape, in the park—is another way to consciously show devotion to this goddess.

In the Roman world, Epona was honored with garlands of roses. These would be draped around her images and even around the necks of horses and mules. Roses—whether actual flowers, or rose-scented candles, perfumes, and the like—can work well to help bring the energy of Epona/Rhiannon into one's life. Another scent, often available as an essential oil, that is useful for connecting with Rhiannon is new-mown hay.

Rhiannon is certainly a goddess of great interest and immediacy for anyone involved with horses. Many people also look to her for protection over other forms of transportation, particularly their cars. This is one way of practicing mindfulness, of bringing awareness of the gods and goddesses into everyday life.

Rhiannon's story shows that another of her aspects is as a deity of marriage and parenthood. It can be extremely helpful not only to appeal to her for marital or family happiness, but also to turn to her when having difficulty with spouse or children. Rhiannon is also a goddess who endures suffering and can be appealed to as a bearer of burdens. She can lend her strength when a difficult task must be undertaken. When we are dealing with loss, particularly the loss of a loved one, she offers not only strength, but also comfort.

There are great depths to Rhiannon, and the mysteries embedded in her story can be contemplated for years. She is the Great Queen of the Otherworld and the Lady of the Sacred Earth. Even as we appeal for her presence in our everyday lives—her assistance with our problems, her blessing on our relationships—she embodies these greater energies as well, and invites us to see the deeper meanings of all we do.

Chapter 11

Ceridwen: Keeper of the Cauldron

The Welsh goddess Ceridwen's name has been translated in various ways: "fair and loved," "perfect love," "crooked woman," "fortress of wisdom," "white song." Some Welsh sources give her name as Graidwen, incorporating an archaic word that can mean "heat," "anger," "bravery," or "fighting." She has been regarded as a figure both beautiful and frightening—a goddess of the earth; of harvest; of magic; of wisdom, poetry, and inspiration; of death and rebirth; of initiation and transformation. Here is her story:

Ceridwen lived with her husband, Tegid the Bald, at the Lake of Tegid in north Wales. They had two children. Their daughter, Creirwy (meaning "light," "beautiful," or "lively treasure"), came to be known as one of the Three Fair Maidens of the Island of Britain. Morfran ("great raven"), their son, was said to have been so ugly that he was called Afagddu, "utter darkness." He was covered with coarse hair, so that people thought he looked like a stag or a demon.

Because of Morfran's appearance, Ceridwen worried that he would have great difficulty making his way in the world and taking his proper place among the noble warriors of Britain. She decided to use her knowledge and her arts to create a potion that would give him wisdom and the spirit of prophecy. At the proper days and at the proper times, she gathered all the necessary herbs, and put them into a cauldron of water. The potion had to be boiled for a year and a day. During this time, Ceridwen kept busy continually gathering and adding more herbs, as well as pouring in fresh water. She had an old blind man and a lad named Gwion Bach ("Little Gwion") to feed the fire under the cauldron and to stir the brew.

At the end of the year and a day, Ceridwen positioned Morfran beside the cauldron to await the three precious drops of potion that were due to spring forth; they would contain all the concentrated virtue of the herbs, and whoever they landed on would receive the gifts of wisdom and prophecy. At the last moment, however, Gwion Bach shoved Morfran out of the way and received the three drops instead. The cauldron itself cried out at this and shattered.

Gwion fled, with Ceridwen in hot pursuit. Gwion turned himself into a hare, that he might run faster, but Ceridwen became a greyhound. Coming to a stream, Gwion took the form of a fish; Ceridwen pursued him as an otter. Gwion took to the air as a bird, and Ceridwen turned herself into a hawk. At last, Gwion changed into a single grain of wheat, concealed in a pile of grain upon a threshing floor. Then Ceridwen became a great black hen. She scratched and pecked at all the wheat until she found the transformed Gwion, whom she swallowed down.

The seed grew in Ceridwen's womb, and nine months later she gave birth to a baby boy. She did not want to raise him, but he was so beautiful that she could not bear to destroy him. So she put him into a little coracle or hide-covered basket-boat, and set him adrift on the waters. Soon he would be found and begin a new life as Taliesin, the archpoet of Britain (about whom we will have more to say in Chapter 21).

Transformation and Inspiration

There is a great deal of magic in this tale, and many people see Ceridwen as the archetypal witch—a crone knowledgeable in arcane secrets, brewing mysterious potions in her cauldron. According to Patrick K. Ford's 1997 translation of "The Tale of Gwion Bach," "she was a magician...and learned in the three arts: magic, enchantment, and divination." The Scottish harper, storyteller, and bardic scholar Robin Williamson prefers to call Ceridwen "a woman of power."

While Ceridwen can certainly be regarded as a powerful witch, the story clearly portrays her as a mother, not as a crone or hag. She is a mature woman, perhaps, but not yet out of her childbearing years. On the other hand, one of the poems attributed to Taliesin, "The Casualties of the Bard," refers to Ceridwen as "a smiling black old hag."[1] The Welsh word usually translated "hag" when referring to Ceridwen is *gwrach,* which also means "witch," "magician," "diviner," and "enchantress"—as well as "ugly old woman." So is Ceridwen a mother or a crone? She can be both—as a goddess of (among other things) birth and death, it is possible for her to take either role, as circumstances require. And this goddess, too, is a shapeshifter.

Shapeshifting is common in Celtic mythology. The transformations in the tale of Ceridwen and Gwion Bach carry the protagonists on a journey through the elements of earth (greyhound and hare), water (otter and fish), and air (hawk and bird). Then Gwion becomes a seed—that essential concentration of life force, holding the potential of all that one may become. And Ceridwen? She is now the devourer, a death force counterposed to the life force in the seed. As the poem "The Hostile Confederacy" says (in John Matthews's translation), speaking in Taliesin's voice, "The Harvester took me,/To free my essence...."

Death, of course, is transformation. A "dead" seed can be buried in the earth, where it receives the nurture it needs to germinate, to open and release the life of a new plant. In the same way, by devouring Gwion Bach, Ceridwen begins the process of preparing him for rebirth into a new life. She is the earth that both buries and nurtures the seed; she is also the crucible where the old is broken down and remade into the new.

This image of the crucible brings us back to Ceridwen's cauldron, one of many magical cauldrons in Celtic lore. Two others prominent in Welsh tradition are the Cauldron of Annwn and the Cauldron of Rebirth. The first of these is described (in the poem "The Spoils of Annwn") as pearl-rimmed and warmed by the breath of nine maidens; it would not boil meat for a coward or for one foresworn—that is, one who had broken his or her word. The Cauldron of Rebirth plays a central role in the Second Branch of the Mabinogi. Its power is that a dead warrior placed within it will be able to rise up ready to fight again—but without the power of speech. Notice how speech and the power of the word are connected with both these cauldrons.

Ceridwen's cauldron is the Cauldron of Inspiration. The Welsh term used for "inspiration"—specifically, poetic inspiration—in relation to the Cauldron is *awen.* Many medieval Welsh poets made statements in their works along the lines of "I received *awen* from the Cauldron of Ceridwen." Sometimes *awen* is translated as "the muse," but this does not adequately convey the nature of *awen,* the power of inspired speech. This Otherworld gift is bestowed on humans in often unexpected fashion, and its demands are great. A person who truly receives the *awen* will never be the same; he or she will be pursued by Ceridwen, who insists that we embrace our divine essence and give it voice.

The Great Sow

Along with her other aspects, Ceridwen has sometimes been called a sow goddess—specifically, the Great Sow who eats her young. Documentation for this view is not as abundant as one might like, but the connection is worth examining. Looking first at actual animal behavior, it can be noted that mother pigs are known to be quite fierce, even deadly. Turning to mythology, in many European religious traditions sows are animals closely associated with the earth and with the underworld. Celtic lore contains numerous references to pork as the meat eaten at Otherworld feasts (and often cooked, by the way, in a cauldron). Continuing this underworld/ Otherworld theme, in the Fourth Branch of the Mabinogi domestic pigs are said to be a gift from Annwn.

The surviving Welsh lore tells of two sows of particular significance. One, described in Triad 26 ("Three Powerful Swineherds of the Island of Britain"), is Henwen, "Old White." Huge and ferocious, she roamed through Cornwall and Wales while pregnant. In one part of south Wales, she gave birth to a grain of wheat and a bee, making that region ever afterward famous for its wheat and honey. She gave birth to a grain of barley in another area, which from then on was the best place for growing barley. In the mountains of north Wales she became the mother of a wolf, an eagle, and a monstrous cat; the eagle and wolf were given to two noblemen— "and they were both the worse for them"—while the cat was thrown into the sea, swam to Anglesey, and went on (according to a fragment of poetry) to kill nine score fierce warriors. Henwen, we see, is an agent of abundance and danger, creation and destruction.

The other notable sow appears in the Fourth Branch. Lleu Llaw Gyffes, terribly injured, has transformed into an eagle and flown away. His foster father, Gwydion, has been searching for him without any luck until he stays the night in a peasant's house. There he learns that the family has a sow who goes out every morning, returning only at night to nurse her piglets. Gwydion follows her, and she leads him to a great oak tree. At its foot she feeds not on acorns, as normal pigs do, but on the rotting flesh of Lleu Llaw Gyffes. Still an eagle, he is perched in the oak's topmost branches.

Gwydion then utters a spontaneous, inspired poem to call Lleu down to him and return him to human form. (For more about Lleu and Gwydion, see Chapters 16 and 19.)

With these two sows, we do indeed see some of the characteristics of Ceridwen. There are the associations with grain, poetry, birth, death, and transformation. Can we say that Henwen and the sow in the Fourth Branch "are" Ceridwen? That may be a matter for further study and meditation. But it is probably not going too far to regard these sows as expressions, at least in part, of Ceridwen's energies at work.

Ceridwen at the Holy Days

Through her association with grain, and specifically its threshing, Ceridwen can be connected with the autumn harvest. Her possible relationship to pigs also points to this time of year, for in much of Western Europe pigs were herded into the woods in October to eat acorns and beechnuts. This leads us to consider Ceridwen as a goddess of Nos Calan Gaeaf, the "Eve of the First Day of Winter" (Halloween/Samhain), considered the final harvest and the beginning of the dark half of the year.

Some Wiccan traditions regard Imbolc (February 1) as a day dedicated to initiation—commemorating the initiation of the young god and/or conducting rituals of initiation or dedication for group members. In either case, Ceridwen may be looked to as the presiding deity of the day. One of the ways of understanding her pursuit and devouring of Gwion Bach is as a mythologized version of the training and initiation rituals undergone by Welsh bards (poet-singers). Moreover, the word *Imbolc* can be interpreted to mean "in the belly" or "in the womb"—not only does Gwion Bach complete his transformation in Ceridwen's womb, but her cauldron itself is a type of womb.

In Wales, Imbolc is usually called Gwyl Fair y Canhwyllau (the Feast of Mary of the Candles) or by similar names relating it to Mary (but sometimes to Brigit—Ffraed in Welsh). Some customs in north Wales for this day, recorded during the 18th and 19th centuries, honor Mary and her child at least on the surface, but might also be seen as carrying forward threads of older traditions. Groups of singers would go door to door and engage in poetic contests with the residents of the houses. Often the singers and the people of the house drank wassail together from a bowl with lit candles around its rim. It is difficult not to be reminded of Ceridwen's cauldron!

Every Day with Ceridwen

Ceridwen is a goddess who expects a great deal from us. She pushes us to be our best and forces us to strip away all that obscures our true nature. But as Ceridwen's pursuit of Gwion Bach shows, reaching one's truest, most magical and gods-aware self can be an uncomfortable and even frightening process.

Inviting Ceridwen's energies into one's life is not a step to be taken lightly. On the other hand, sometimes this is the step we need to take—and if we don't, our life circumstances will probably give us a push (or more than one!) down the path.

"Know thyself" has long been a motto of many mystery religions, and it certainly applies to Ceridwen's lessons. An exercise used at the beginning of many systems of magical training is commonly called the Black and White Mirror, and it would make an appropriate first step in working with the energies of Ceridwen, who is mother of both light and darkness. The exercise has several variations; here is one:

Get a small notebook that you can carry with you wherever you go, and use it for nothing but this exercise. For one week, write down all of your negative qualities—every characteristic or tendency that you can think of that keeps you from being the best person you could be. For the next week, think over those qualities and rate them on a scale of one to three, depending on how much they impact you. For example, if you lose your temper frequently, you might rate anger as a three; if you tell a little white lie once in a while, you would probably rate dishonesty as a one. These two weeks can be extremely uncomfortable—but the next two weeks are actually harder for many people. Now you will spend a week listing all your positive qualities, the things you like about yourself. The next week, of course, you will rate them. Finally, take a week or two (but no more) to look at the patterns in your qualities. Analyze them according to the elements through which Ceridwen pursued Gwion Bach: earth (the body, the five senses, physical needs), water (emotions), and air (the mind, intellect, ideas). If you prefer working with a four-element system, you can add fire, which stands primarily for the will.

At the end of this exercise you will know yourself much better and will see where you have imbalances that you can work on remedying. You will also see that your faults and your strengths are often two sides of the same coin; for example, stubbornness and persistence are basically the same quality, differing mainly in how it is applied in life situations. By the way, there are no "right answers" in this exercise, but only individual answers. Looking again at the previous example, for one person stubbornness may be an earthy quality, but for another it may relate more to fire. Your own understanding of yourself is what's important here, and the willingness to grow. For that reason, many people like to repeat this exercise once a year.

Working to transform yourself into the best conduit of the divine spirit that you can be is probably the most important way to show devotion to Ceridwen. But you can also honor her on a smaller scale. In one of the poems attributed to Taliesin (titled "Defence of the Chair" by John and Caitlín Matthews), the poet speaks of offering Ceridwen milk, dew, and acorns. You might need to substitute springwater for the dew, but otherwise this is an offering that anyone can make. Candles or altar decorations for her can be in black, red, and white. A small cauldron with a candle in it makes an excellent focus for beginning to meditate on the mysteries of Ceridwen. But if you do nothing else for Ceridwen, cultivate your enjoyment of poetry. Recite it, read it aloud, or sing it. And if the *awen* comes to you, let your own poetry and songs flow.

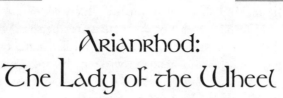

Chapter 12

Arianrhod:
The Lady of the Wheel

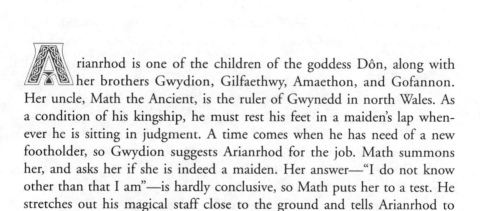

Arianrhod is one of the children of the goddess Dôn, along with her brothers Gwydion, Gilfaethwy, Amaethon, and Gofannon. Her uncle, Math the Ancient, is the ruler of Gwynedd in north Wales. As a condition of his kingship, he must rest his feet in a maiden's lap whenever he is sitting in judgment. A time comes when he has need of a new footholder, so Gwydion suggests Arianrhod for the job. Math summons her, and asks her if she is indeed a maiden. Her answer—"I do not know other than that I am"—is hardly conclusive, so Math puts her to a test. He stretches out his magical staff close to the ground and tells Arianrhod to step over it. As she does, she "drops" a yellow-haired boy, whom Math later names Dylan and who goes to live in the sea.

Arianrhod keeps right on walking, but as she is about to go out the door, she drops something else. Only Gwydion sees it. He scoops it up and hides it in a chest at the foot of his bed. Time passes until, one morning, he is awakened by a noise coming from the chest. Opening it, he finds a baby boy. The child grows twice as fast, in body and mind, as ordinary boys. When he is 4 years old, Gwydion takes him to Arianrhod's seaside fortress to meet his mother.

It is not a particularly happy reunion. First, Arianrhod scolds Gwydion for disgracing her by keeping the boy for so long. Then, when she asks what his name is, Gwydion tells her that he has not yet got a name. "Well," says Arianrhod, "and he will not have a name unless he gets it from me." Gwydion and the boy leave, but the next day Gwydion uses his magical arts to disguise the two of them as shoemakers. He conjures a ship out of seaweed, and they sail into the harbor below Arianrhod's fortress. There they set about making shoes of beautiful gilded leather. Arianrhod goes down to the ship to have a pair of shoes made for herself. While Gwydion is measuring her foot, a wren, the smallest of birds, alights on the deck. In a flash, the boy casts his shoemaker's awl at it, hitting its leg. Arianrhod smiles and declares, "*Lleu llaw gyffes!*" —"A bright one with a skillful hand!" From his mother's words, the boy's name becomes Lleu Llaw Gyffes.

Then Arianrhod says, "Now I swear, he will never take arms till I arm him myself." Gwydion takes Lleu home and continues to raise him. The years pass; Lleu grows and matures. At last it is time that a youth of his age and station should take arms, so Gwydion disguises the two of them as bards, and they head for Arianrhod's fortress, where they are welcomed eagerly and shown great hospitality.

After feasting, Gwydion and Arianrhod tell tales and recite lore. Later, while all the court sleeps, Gwydion works his magic so that, when dawn comes, a huge fleet of ships appears to be anchored just off the coast, with warriors pouring ashore. Arianrhod comes to Gwydion and Lleu's room to ask for their help in defending the castle. They agree, but because neither of the "bards" has arms or weapons, Arianrhod and two maidens fetch what is needed from the castle stores.

"Lady," says Gwydion, "let the maidens help me arm, and you assist the young man." She does this gladly, and when Lleu is fully armed, weapons in hand, Gwydion lifts all his enchantments.

"So he has his name and his arms," says Arianrhod. "But I swear this destiny: He will never find a wife among the people now on this earth." Gwydion declares that he will get Lleu a wife all the same—but we will leave that part of the tale for Chapter 16.

This story of Arianrhod, her brother, and her son is found in the Fourth Branch of the Mabinogi. Some fragments of Welsh poetry suggest that other versions of the tale were known during the Middle Ages—in one, it seems, Arianrhod did in fact become Math's footholder and companion. We also find Arianrhod mentioned in some of the Triads; one of them states that she had two other sons (besides Dylan and Lleu), whose father was Lliaws mab Nwyfre, and that her father was Beli Mawr, regarded as the divine ancestor of early Welsh kings. Medieval Welsh poets spoke of Arianrhod as "famous for beauty" and "a pure, white-armed wise one."

In the Fortress of Arianrhod

Arianrhod means "silver wheel." Many manuscript sources, however, give her name as Aranrhod, probably meaning "great wheel." Either way, "wheel" is a major element of her name and, we assume, her identity.[1] So what might be the significance of this wheel?

"Silver wheel" suggests right off an association with the moon. Welsh tradition also makes a connection between Arianrhod and the stars. In Welsh, the constellation widely known as Corona Borealis or the Northern Crown is called Caer Arianrhod—"the Fortress (or Castle) of Arianrhod." Other members of her family, too, are commemorated in the heavens: The Welsh name for the constellation Cassiopeia is Llys Dôn, "the Court of Dôn," while the Milky Way is Caer Gwydion. The name of Arianrhod's husband in the Triads means "Multitude, son of Sky," also seeming to refer to the stars.

Let's now look closer at Caer Arianrhod. There are three ways we can understand it: earthly, celestial, and Otherworldly. The earthly Caer was said to be on the northeast coast of Wales, and indeed there is a rock about a mile offshore, visible only at low tide, that is traditionally known as Caer Arianrhod. The celestial Caer is, of course, in the stars. Both of these are, in a sense, signposts to the Otherworld Caer Arianrhod, for neither a fortress in the night sky nor one at the edge of or under the sea are completely of this world.

The Otherworld Caer is a place of changes and transformations. When Lleu visits the earthly fortress of Arianrhod, he also crosses into the Otherworldly realm: On the physical level he receives a name and arms, while on the spiritual level he is transformed from boy to youth and then from youth to man, with all of the qualities and responsibilities that belong to those states. Also, it is in Caer Arianrhod that his destiny is decreed.

On the surface, Arianrhod is one who sets up barriers and obstacles. Looking into deeper meanings of her story, however, we can see that she is actually a tester and a facilitator of change—that is, an initiator. Just as Ceridwen can be seen as an initiator of poets and prophets, we might understand Arianrhod as an initiator of warriors and leaders. She sets or-deals to test the candidate and makes sure that circumstances are right for the crossing from one state of life to the next. Her son does not receive his adult name until he can demonstrate that he is ready for it through a deed that shows his quality. He does not receive his arms until it is clear that he will fight to protect others. And neither name nor arms can come from anyone save his mother. We can summarize this as a triad:

Three things essential to a leader:

> a name for deeds,
> a will to defend the defenseless,
> and mindfulness of life's source.

Arianrhod's declaration that Lleu will never have a wife from among the people now in this world is open to a variety of interpretations—we'll look at some of them in Chapter 16. Here, let's consider the possibility that Arianrhod is not imposing a "taboo" on her son, but simply uttering the truth. She knows that, being who and what he is, Lleu is not going to be able to marry any ordinary woman. Arianrhod is telling him his fate.

The notion of fate brings us around again to the Great Wheel, and we may sense resonances between this Welsh myth and strands of myth and philosophy from other times and places. Think of Fortune's Wheel, of the starry wheel of the zodiac, of karma and the Wheel of Rebirth—all expressing concepts of destiny and possibilities of transformation.

During the period of Roman rule in Britain and Gaul, the native Celts adopted Roman religious concepts that harmonized with traditional ideas. Among these, the Celts sometimes identified their trio of goddesses called the Mothers (see Chapter 4) with the three Fates, and they adopted the Roman goddess Fortuna, the personification of luck and chance. Fortuna's symbols, which show up from time to time in Romano-British (as well as Gallo-Roman) sculptures of native goddesses, are the cornucopia, the rudder, the globe—and the wheel. Arianrhod, we remember, pronounces a triple fate on her son, and the symbol from which she takes her name is the wheel. Roman influence, long forgotten and thoroughly incorporated into British tradition, may be at play here, but in any case it seems clear that fate and fortune are among Arianrhod's principal concerns.

In one of the poems attributed to him, Taliesin (see Chapter 21) speaks of a "dear one" being held "below" in "the fetters of Arianrhod." It is possible that this refers to karma, the chain of cause and effect that creates an individual's fate. Taliesin himself has, he asserts in another poem, been three times in Arianrhod's castle or prison. Because of the context of the poem, Caer Arianrhod here can be understood as a place of death and rebirth—perhaps metaphorically, as a place of initiation (which involves a symbolic death and rebirth), and/or more literally as a place where the soul resides between lifetimes. A third interpretation is that the "prison" could refer to incarnation itself—it is during our human lives, after all, that we are "chained" by the operations of cause and effect.

As we contemplate the nature of Arianrhod and her Caer, two other poems attributed to Taliesin contain passages worth considering. In "The Chair of Ceridwen," Arianrhod is said to throw out a rainbow to encircle her court and protect it from attack. "The Spoils of Annwn" tells of a voyage to the Otherworld, where one of its "regions" is called Caer Sidi. *Sidi* means "spiral" or "turning," and some people think this is another name for Caer Arianrhod—the Silver Wheel always spinning. Is the rainbow perhaps the shimmering veil of sensory perception, separating this world from the Otherworld? Yet it is a world that may be touched and even visited—during death or dreams or visions or initiation—and there are some, like Taliesin, who can remember and tell about it afterward.

Arianrhod and Sacred Time

The dark of the moon, when the stars shine most brightly, lends itself well to meditating on the mysteries of Arianrhod. The full moon is a wonderful time to honor her more actively. This can be as simple as going out under the moonlight and raising a toast or blowing a kiss to the Silver Wheel, or as elaborate as a group ritual with circular or spiral dancing.

In the Fourth Branch of the Mabinogi, Arianrhod is a maiden who gives birth to a child of light, so Yuletide can be regarded as her season. She also presides over the Bright One's coming of age. For this reason, some Wiccan traditions grounded in Welsh mythology invoke her at Spring Equinox when, speaking metaphorically, the sun is crossing from childhood into youth.

Every Day with Arianrhod

Arianrhod is a "hard mother"—and there are times when every parent has to be hard on a child. It doesn't feel good! Arianrhod's energy can help us with those times when we must make our children do uncomfortable, difficult, or even painful things that are for their own good—whether it's a visit to the doctor, a troublesome homework assignment, or a serious discipline issue.

We might also be mindful of Arianrhod when we encounter obstacles in our lives. Many times, what seems like a roadblock is really just a test or challenge, and we will be stronger and more capable for having worked our way through it. Arianrhod also reminds us that behind everything that befalls us, there is a reason—even if we cannot see it. "Fate" doesn't so much mean that our destiny is written in the stars, but that we enter this life with a set of potentials, for both good and bad. The circumstances and events of our early childhood interact with those potentials to shape us in certain ways. Then, increasingly, our decisions and actions will determine the route our life's path takes. Fate, or karma—the chain of cause and effect—is always at work beneath the surface of our lives, on the other side of the veil, in Caer Arianrhod.

There are many ways to connect with Arianrhod and become more mindful of her energies. Silver, of course, is her color; wheels, circles, stars, and spirals can all be used as symbols for her. Any movement in a circular fashion may be done with the intent of connecting with Arianrhod. If you have access to a spinning wheel or even a drop spindle, spinning can be a wonderfully meditative activity under the aegis of Arianrhod.

And do pay attention to the moon and stars. If you're inclined to study astronomy or astrology in depth, that's wonderful. But it's even more important to simply look up into the sky for at least a few minutes every night. Observe the phases of the moon. Learn to recognize some of the constellations.[2] Simply enjoy the immeasurable beauty spread out above us. Everything in the universe is in motion, and we are a part of the whole. From incredible distances, the light of the moon and stars reaches us—the touch of the goddess, if we choose to see it that way. In the words of Starhawk's classic chant, "She changes everything she touches, and everything she touches changes."

Part Three:
Gods and Heroes

Chapter 13

Cernunnos: Master of the Hunt

ernunnos is widely known today as the Horned God worshipped in many Wiccan traditions. *Cernunnos*, in fact, means "Horned One" in Gaulish, and images of a god with horns or antlers have been found in many parts of the Celtic world, especially Gaul. For the most part, however, these images do not include the god's name (or names). A single relief from Paris records the name or title Cernunnos. Beneath the inscription is an image of the god as a mature, bearded man with deer's ears and antlers; hanging on each antler is a torc (a neck ring typically worn by Celtic men and women of high status). It has become common practice to refer to all otherwise unnamed antlered Celtic gods as Cernunnos—for even though these deities may have been referred to differently among the various tribes that worshipped them, it seems clear that they all shared the same divine attributes.

The oldest depiction of Cernunnos comes from northern Italy, an area once thickly settled by Celts. This image is a rock carving, probably made in the fourth century B.C.E. It shows an antlered male wearing a long robe and a torc on each arm. Accompanying him are a ram-horned snake and a small man with erect penis. This imagery makes it clear that virility and fertility were among the god's concerns. The ram-horned snake is also associated with these qualities and, in addition, symbolizes the underworld and the power of regeneration.

Cernunnos was frequently depicted with torcs and a ram-horned snake, most famously on the Gundestrup Cauldron. This silver ritual bowl (about

14 inches high and 25.5 inches in diameter) was made in the first century B.C.E., probably by Thracian silversmiths working for Celtic patrons. In a scene on the Cauldron's inner surface, Cernunnos sits cross-legged, wearing one torc and holding another. With his left hand, he grasps a ram-horned snake. Immediately to his right is a stag, with whom he is clearly identified—stag and god have identical antlers. Other animals accompany them, interspersed with stylized leafy plants. Here Cernunnos appears very much as a lord of the beasts, a god of wild nature.

Both these images of Cernunnos date to before the Roman invasions of Celtic territory. Such pre-Roman depictions of Celtic deities are quite rare. After the Roman conquest, however, Roman sculptural techniques were adopted and adapted, and the stone reliefs and statues of goddesses and gods clearly show the influence of the Greco-Roman artistic tradition. But in the 50-plus known images of Cernunnos produced during the Roman period (many of them from northeastern Gaul), the god's native Celtic attributes stand out.

Along with the torcs and ram-horned snakes, the god's usual posture is distinctively Celtic. He is generally portrayed squatting or sitting cross-legged (as the Greco-Roman gods were not). According to several classical authors, the Celts of Gaul typically sat or squatted on the ground; they did not use chairs. It may be, then, that Cernunnos's posture is meant to reflect a kind of commonality with his worshippers.

The torc that Cernunnos often holds could indicate the abundance and prosperity that he provides. This aspect of the god appears very clearly in some of the Roman-period sculptures. For instance, in a relief from Reims, France, he has a large bag in his lap. Out of it pour coins, and on either side of this cascade stand a bull and a stag. A plaque from Cirencester in Britain shows Cernunnos with what appear to be open purses on each side of him, below his antlers; in each hand he holds a ram-horned snake.

All these images of Cernunnos together give the impression of a beneficent and powerful deity who seems to be equally at home among humans and animals—in fact, in himself he forms a link between those two worlds. At the same time, he has affinities with the underworld or Otherworld, connecting him with both death and regeneration. And he is a giver of wealth—whether in the form of abundant game, cattle, or money.

Julius Caesar wrote that the Celts of Gaul believed themselves to be descended from Dis Pater, the Roman name for the lord of death and the underworld, who was also the source of all abundance. It may well be that the god Caesar had in mind was none other than Cernunnos.

On the Path of the Horned One

There is no existing myth about Cernunnos—under that name. It is possible, however, that English folklore concerning Herne the Hunter kept alive some memories of Cernunnos—although by Shakespeare's time Herne's character was rather sinister. In Act IV of *The Merry Wives of Windsor*, Herne (whose name probably comes from the same root as *Cernunnos*) is closely associated with cattle—but not in a positive way:

> There is an old tale goes that Herne the hunter,
> Sometime a keeper here in Windsor Forest,
> Doth all the winter time at still midnight
> Walk round about an oak with great ragg'd horns;
> And there he blasts the trees, and takes the cattle,
> And makes milch-kine yield blood, and shakes a chain
> In a most hideous and dreadful manner.

A similar figure in Welsh lore is Gwyn ap Nudd. In "Culhwch and Olwen" he is a renowned huntsman who has authority in Annwn. Medieval poetry depicts him as a spirit who lurks on battlefields and escorts the dead to the Otherworld. In more recent folklore, he has been regarded as king of the Fairy Folk and leader of the Wild Hunt.

Turning back to the Mabinogi, we meet a deity who may be identified even more closely with Cernunnos: Arawn, Chief of Annwn. At the beginning of the First Branch, Pwyll, lord of Dyfed, goes hunting one day. With his dogs, he follows a white stag that leads him deeper and deeper into the forest till they reach a clearing that has never been there before. As they arrive on the scene, another pack of hounds—white with red ears—comes from the opposite direction and brings down the stag. Pwyll drives them off and lets his own dogs feast on the kill. A moment later, into the clearing rides a huntsman all in gray, on a great gray horse. He chides Pwyll for dishonorably claiming the prey that was another's—his—and Pwyll, admitting to his failing, offers to pay the stranger's honor price.

The huntsman reveals that he is Arawn, Chief of Annwn, and demands that he and Pwyll switch places for a year and a day, at the end of which Pwyll must do battle with Arawn's enemy Hafgan ("Summer-Bright"). The switch is made, and Arawn even shifts his shape to Pwyll's and changes Pwyll's to his. Each goes to govern the other's realm.

Pwyll finds Annwn to be the fairest land imaginable—and Arawn's wife the fairest woman imaginable. But out of honor, he never so much as speaks to Arawn's wife when they are in bed together at night, though he is courteous to her at all other times.

At the end of the year and a day, Pwyll defeats Hafgan in single combat, then returns to the clearing where he first met Arawn. The Chief of Annwn restores them each to their own shape, and each returns to his land. Both are pleased to find how well the other has governed in his absence. But Arawn is even more pleased when his wife tells him of Pwyll's behavior toward her. Arawn rewards Pwyll for his honor and loyalty with a vow of everlasting friendship between Annwn and Dyfed. As the mark of this friendship, Arawn enriches Dyfed by the regular gifts that he sends to Pwyll from Annwn. Pwyll, for his part, sends Arawn such presents as he thinks will please him.

In this story, we see Arawn as a lord of the Otherworld; as a master of animals and the hunt, closely linked with the stag; and as an enricher of humanity—all attributes of Cernunnos. His interaction with Pwyll, then, shows us some of the ways in which we might show devotion to the Horned One. Above all, we are expected to act with honor, never claiming that which does not belong to us and always following through on our given word. At the same time, we should be daring, unafraid to follow the white stag, even though we know it will lead us into the unknown and unexpected.

What we encounter in that new clearing in the forest to which the stag leads us will change our lives forever if we let it. We are given the opportunity to prove ourselves worthy of the gifts of the Otherworld, the true abundance that enriches not just our own life, but also the lives of those around us. We will see the presence of the Otherworld and this world in one another, knowing the sacredness of the land where we walk, and act with a generosity that honors the source of bounty. So we become friends of the Otherworld and its mighty and generous lord.

Listen for the horn that summons you to the hunt....

Chapter 14

The Dagda: The Big Father

Back in the days when gods and goddesses lived aboveground in Ireland, a great conflict emerged between the Túatha Dé Danann and their archenemies, the Fomorians. The Fomorians were a fearsome tribe of misshapen evil spirits who were said to live on an island off the west coast of Éire—although some bards even hinted that they lived under the water, demons of the deep. So when the time came for battle between the Tribes of the Goddess Dana and these fearsome beings, it was clear that the Túatha Dé would need to muster every skill, every ability, every resource at their command.

For their leader, the Túatha Dé turned to Lugh, a radiant young deity who embodied light and skill and protection (and who is the subject of Chapter 16). When Lugh took command at the great hall of Tara, he promptly demonstrated his leadership ability, inspiring every member of the community to step forward with their best skills for defeating the enemy. Various of the Túatha Dé made promises: Goibhniu the smith pledged to make magical spears that would never miss their mark; the Morrigán declared that she would instill fear in the hearts of all the enemy; and Dian Cécht the physician promised to heal the warriors who fell in battle, so long as their heads were not severed from their bodies. Finally, the Dagda spoke: "These great things that all of you are boasting you will do, I can do them all as well, all by myself!" Everyone cheered and acclaimed him the "Good God"—good at all things, not unlike their champion, Lugh, master of all the skills.

Lugh may have been called "master of all skills" (Samildánach), but the Dagda had his own unique epithets. These include "great father of all" (Eochaidh Ollathair), "mighty one of perfect knowledge" (Ruad Rofhessa), and "red eye" (Deirgderc). These are impressive titles, and yet the Dagda is hardly what most modern people would think of as a champion. Fatter than a sumo wrestler, he seems more a buffoon than a hero; indeed, his distended belly was so huge that his too-small tunic barely covered his buttocks! And whereas Lugh was a deity committed to justice and the protection of his people, the Dagda seemed to be more interested in a huge feast—or a sexual liaison—than in putting his multilayered prowess to use in battle.

This is not to suggest that the Good God was merely some sort of ancient Celtic hippie, committed to making love not war. No, the Dagda did not shrink from battle, and truly had nothing to fear in it. He wielded a mighty club, so heavy that it had to be transported on wheels; it was said that he could slay nine men with a single blow. Even more amazing was the club's handle—for just as the club end could wield death, if the Dagda touched the handle to a slain warrior, it would restore him to life.

In addition to his miraculous club, this clownish god owned two other great magical possessions: a harp that could fly to his hand when he called for it and a cauldron, said to be one of the four great treasures of the Túatha Dé Danann, that could feed an entire army. The ladle for his cauldron was large enough to hold a man and a woman (a description that may well be a fertility image—large enough to hold a mating couple). The Dagda also possessed two magical swine, one always being fattened for the slaughter and the other always on the spit being cooked; he likewise had ever-laden fruit trees.

Larger than Life

The theme that emerges for the Dagda is "larger than life." He's not just a father god; he is the ultimate provider and the guardian of death and life. As a paternal deity, he is a dad not in a stern, angry, judgmental sense (as God the Father is portrayed in some forms of Christianity) or in a capricious, I'm-above-the-law arrogant sense (like Zeus of the Greek pantheon). Rather, the Dagda is more of a big, jolly, happy, loving, and yet slightly ridiculous (but very much on top of things) kind of a dad. Think Jerry Garcia meets Santa Claus.

The Dagda's megabuild is hardly unique to the world of mythology—but huge deities often seem to be female rather than male. So many of the earliest archaeological treasures that represent prehistoric goddesses depict them as the opposite of anorexic; goddesses like the "Venus" of Willendorf are fleshy and corpulent, expressing their role as givers of abundance and fertility in—pardon the pun—a big way. The Dagda comes out of this same tradition. Only he is a *god* of abundance, who manifests his generous prosperity through his bulging masculine physique.

Of course, one of the qualities associated with a big girth is a super-sized appetite. This aspect of the Good God contributes to the humor of another tale told about him. Just before the climactic battle of Mag Tuired, when the full fury of the Fomorians would be unleashed against the Túatha Dé, Lugh sent the Dagda to spy on the enemy camp. He presented himself as an emissary, asking for a delay in the battle, and the Fomorians agreed. But finding this ambassador of the gods to be utterly ridiculous in his appearance, the enemy decided to set him up for an insult. Strict codes of hospitality meant that it would have been an unforgivable breach of etiquette for the Dagda, as a visitor, to refuse any food offered to him. With this in mind, the Fomorians dug a huge pit in the ground, filling it not only with milk, porridge, and broth, but also with huge cuts of pork and beef and mutton. Then they made a fuss over their guest, declaring that this stomach-turning stew had been prepared just for him, and they insisted that he eat every bite. After all, they would not allow it to be said that the Fomorians lacked hospitality (an ironic concern, as their reputation for niggardliness was already worse than awful). Indeed, they offered their so-called hospitality with an unmistakable threat: "We will make an end of you if you leave any part of it behind," said the Fomorian Indech with more than a hint of malice in his tone.

Taken aback not at all, the Dagda asked for a ladle and proceeded to engorge himself on the pitful of food. He scraped the pit so thoroughly that at the end he was chewing on the gravel and soil from its bottom. Eventually he dozed off, and the Fomorians made great fun of him before sleep overtook them as well. But he had the last laugh: When he awoke, he seduced a Fomorian princess before leaving their camp.

A Lusty God

This brings us to another quality of this massive god: a prodigious sexuality. Like his appetite and his physique, the Dagda's exuberant ability to enjoy the pleasures of various and sundry lovers is not about moral turpitude, but is rather a part of his function as an archetype of fertility and prosperity. As he makes love to various goddesses, so he symbolizes the sacred spark that ignites new life throughout the universe.

One of the most famous stories about the Dagda as a lover involves the Morrigán. The Good God is traveling to an important council where the Túatha Dé Danann will discuss their strategy against the Fomorians. Upon reaching the Unshin River, the Dagda notes to his aroused surprise that the great Phantom Queen is bathing herself, with one foot planted on either bank of the river. Gazing up at her vulva, the Dagda wastes no time in propositioning the fearsome goddess, and is rewarded with a vigorous coupling. Afterward, the Morrigán prophesies concerning the forthcoming battle—and the victory the Túatha Dé will enjoy. This event takes place on the festival of Samhain—the dark holiday when the goddess of battle and death mates with a god of life and abundance, thereby renewing the sacred cosmos for another year.

And so Samhain is particularly sacred to the Dagda, both because of its harvest connections and his role as the lover of the goddess of death. But he is a god who could just as easily be venerated at any time during the year. The dual nature of his club (as a force for death and life) makes him a fitting deity to be honored on the Spring and Fall Equinoxes—even though there is no ancient reason to link him with those dates, because we have no firm evidence that the Celts honored the equinoxes at all. But from a Neo-Pagan perspective of venerating the concept of balance on those two days, the Dagda certainly qualifies as a god who exhibits many kinds of "balances"—the obese buffoon who is also a fearsome warrior; the father who is also a lover; the bringer of death who simultaneously is the restorer of life.

The Spirituality of the Dagda

What can we learn from the Dagda? More than anything, that there is a link between skill and abundance—but whereas Lugh represents skill in its purest form, the Dagda's excellence is more earthy, erotic, humble, and humorous. He knows he is ridiculous and, far from being bothered by it, actually takes delight in his own oafishness. After all, so much abundance flows through him that he lacks for nothing: not even silliness!

The Dagda may seem an unlikely partner for a figure as dark and terrible as the Morrigán, and yet, as a warrior of death and a god of fertility, he represents the dark earth in contrast to Lugh's rarefied status as a solar/light deity. Lugh's son Cú Chulainn stupidly rejects the powerful chthonic sexuality of the Morrigán, but the Dagda makes no such ignorant move. He exults in embracing the Morrigán, symbolically showing that a person truly alive lives with full knowledge of his or her mortality.

How can we honor the Dagda today? By choosing to exult in the good things of life: whether food, or sex, or our own ability to master a skill. But we also honor the Good God when we laugh at our own foibles or when we exhibit old-fashioned self-reliance; after all, he is the god who said, "All that you promise, I will do for myself." Making music (especially on the harp); accepting our bodies, even when we're a bit (or a lot) overweight; and, for men, taking delight in fatherhood are all ways to bring the Dagda's big spirit into our lives. Finally, choosing to believe that the world we live in is one of abundance and prosperity—rather than a place of scarcity and lack—might be the best way to venerate this colorful god.

Chapter 15

Manannán and Manawydan: Lords of the Mist

The Irish Manannán and Welsh Manawydan both, according to scholars, take their name from the Isle of Man (Mannin in Manx, Mana or Manu in Irish, Manaw in Welsh), which lies in the Irish Sea between Britain and Ireland. Manx folklore and legend is full of references to and stories about Mannanan (the Manx spelling of the name), traditionally regarded as the first king of Man and its eternal guardian. The emblem of Man, in fact, is a triskele formed of three legs clad in silver and gold armor— the three magical legs of Mannanan, which can turn into a fiery wheel according to Manx folktales.

Manannán

Among the Irish gods, Manannán is as mysterious as the mist of the sea. He is said to be the son of a shadowy deity named Lir; both father and son are gods of the ocean, although Manannán is far more prominent in Irish lore than his dad. Lir, in fact, is best known for his other children: Fionnula, Aedh, Fiachra, and Conn, who were cursed by their evil stepmother to spend 900 years as swans.

The tradition hints that Manannán may actually be a god far older than the Túatha Dé Danann and, therefore, is not a member of that tribe. As ruler of the sea, he resides on an island called Emain Ablach (a mysterious name the meaning of which is unclear, but it appears to have something to do with apple trees—presumably trees bearing miraculous fruit that bestows immortality on those who eat of it); this island is part of the magical Otherworldly paradise known as Tír Tairnigiri (the Land of Promise).

Like so many Celtic deities, Manannán is a warrior, strong, noble, and handsome. But his godly powers extend beyond the skill of a fighter to include magical prowess as well. Such supernatural skills might cover a wide range of abilities, from hiding behind the ocean mist to traveling across the surface of the sea in a chariot drawn by "horses" made of the waves.

As the sea god, Manannán is both a protector of the land (after all, Ireland's best defense is the fact that it is surrounded by water) and the guardian of the gates between this world and the Otherworld (because after death, it is said, one must travel over the sea to reach the Lands of Youth and Promise). But Manannán's role as guardian of the Otherworld is not confined to activity on the open sea. In one tale, Manannán escorts the semi-historical Irish king Cormac mac Airt from his royal seat at Tara into the Otherworld, passing through the sea god's veil of mist. He brings Cormac to an Otherworldly feast, hosted by the smith god Goibhniu, but at which Manannán presides. This is the feast where the Túatha Dé Danann receive immortality by eating the flesh of Manannán's pigs and drinking Goibhniu's ale. Before escorting the amazed king back into ordinary reality, Manannán gives Cormac the legendary silver branch: a branch of an apple tree, laden with golden fruit, that when shaken can calm all who hear its rustling, musical sound—or, for that matter, can open a doorway to the Otherworld.

Like the Dagda and Lugh, Manannán is a master of many skills—not the least of which are his abilities concerning illusion, magic, and trickery. He wears a great cloak that catches the light and gives forth many colors, almost like the sea itself. Manannán is the possessor of a magic bag made of the skin of a crane, which is said to contain all the treasures of the Túatha Dé Danann.

Manannán also had a reputation as a benefactor of other gods: He bestowed many magical gifts to Lugh to assist him in his quest to vanquish the Fomorians, including a boat that obeyed the thoughts of its sailor and could be navigated without oar or sail, a horse that could travel with equal ease on land or sea, and an unstoppable sword called Fragarach ("the answerer"), which could pierce any armor. To Lugh's son, Cú Chulainn, the sea god gave a magic visor. More poignantly, he also gave Cú Chulainn the gift of forgetfulness, when he had fallen in love with Manannán's fairy wife, Fand ("the pearl of beauty").

As a trickster, Manannán one time decided to seduce a mortal queen whose husband was away at battle. To do this, he appeared to the husband and said that he would fail at battle unless he permitted Manannán, disguised as the king, to sleep with the queen. The king agreed. In another version of the story, he appeared to the queen, telling her that her husband would die in battle unless she welcomed him into her bed. In both versions, the queen became pregnant and gave birth to Mongán, whom Manannán fostered in Tír Tairnigiri and who then returned to Ulster to become a great and renowned warrior—not unlike King Arthur, the British warrior whose conception involved similar intrigue.

Another child of Manannán's who plays an important role in Irish myth is Áine, a love and fertility goddess associated with the sun. She has been renowned both for her vigorous sexual appetite (with a special fondness for mortal men) and for her final role in folklore as a fairy queen.

For the modern seeker of Celtic wisdom, Manannán's importance truly centers on his function as the gatekeeper to the Otherworld. Here in the 21st century, we can think of Manannán as the lord of the vast ocean of the collective unconscious that surrounds the tiny island of our conscious minds. He may be thought of, therefore, as the guardian of the gates that separate our ordinary awareness from altered states of consciousness—especially magical or mystical states. Similarly, as the waves of the sea are Manannán's horses, so the waves of thought and emotion within us represent the surface activity of the inner sea, which, like the oceans of the earth, are far deeper than we may ever know.

The hidden meaning of the Irish lore is this: Through Manannán, the old gods invite us to travel over the ocean that lies beyond the shoreline of ordinary consciousness to find the inner worlds of magic deep within. Such a journey may seem shrouded in mist, mystery, and perhaps a measure of psychic danger. To make the passage safely, Manannán is a sure and valuable guide. It is he to whom we can pray for the grace to travel between the worlds with peace, confidence, and safety—not for thrill seeking or as a "spiritual tourist," but with a reverent heart, knowing that the traveler to the Otherworld is forever changed.

Manawydan

Unlike Manannán, virtually Manawydan's only link with the sea in Welsh tradition is his patronym, Mab Llyr—"Son of the Sea." He is referred to as one of the Three Humble Chieftains because he never sought lands or territories—even those to which he was entitled by birth. At the beginning of the Third Branch of the Mabinogi, in fact, he has no home at all. But, as we have seen in Chapter 10, he goes to live with his friend Pryderi in Dyfed, where he marries Rhiannon. And although Pryderi remains ruler of Dyfed in name, Manawydan assumes the actual governance of the land.

One day after a feast, Rhiannon, Manawydan, Pryderi, and Cigfa (Pryderi's wife) climb the Mound of Arberth. As they sit on the mound, there is a clamorous sound, and a thick mist falls all around them. When it lifts, they see that the land is deserted; the people, herds, flocks, and houses have vanished. In all of Dyfed, only they and the empty court buildings remain.

For the present, there is nothing to be done. After exhausting their stores, the four support themselves on game, fish, and wild honey. After a time, they grow tired of this and of being alone in the land, so Manawydan decides that they should move to England. They settle in a town, where Manawydan, with Pryderi's assistance, begins to make saddles so fine that soon no one will buy from any of the town's other saddlers. The jealous craftsmen plot to kill Manawydan and Pryderi. When Pryderi hears of this, he wants to kill the saddlers. But Manawydan restrains him, counseling that fighting will only make their situation worse.

They leave that town and move to another, where Manawydan sets about making shields. Soon all of the other shield makers are out of business and conspiring to kill Manawydan and Pryderi. Again Pryderi wants to retaliate; again Manawydan advises against violence, and they move on. In the third town, he goes to work as a shoemaker—one of the Three Golden Shoemakers of the Isle of Britain.[1] But the same thing as before happens, so Manawydan decides it would be best for them to return to Dyfed.

Luckily, they've obtained hounds and horses to make their hunting easier, and this is how they survive for some time. Then one day Pryderi and Manawydan follow a white boar through the woods to a fortress that has never been there before. The dogs chase the boar into the fort; Manawydan, sensing something amiss, counsels Pryderi not to follow, but Pryderi will not abandon his hounds.

Within the fortress, Pryderi sees no sign of dogs or boar. In the middle of the courtyard, however, is a fountain. At the fountain's edge is a basin of gold hanging from golden chains that stretch up into the sky. Pryderi takes hold of the basin and immediately finds himself stuck fast, without power of speech or movement. When Manawydan returns home alone, Rhiannon (after scolding him) runs out to find her son—and suffers the same fate as Pryderi. As darkness falls, so does a thick mist. With a loud clattering sound, the fortress disappears, Rhiannon and Pryderi with it.

Manawydan decides it's no use for him and Cigfa to remain where they are. They go to England, where Manawydan again sets himself up as a shoemaker. As before, the other craftsmen became murderously jealous. So Manawydan procures a load of wheat seed, and he and Cigfa return to Dyfed. There he sows three crofts with wheat.

Harvest time comes, and Manawydan goes out to the first croft—to find that each stalk has been broken off and the ear of wheat carried away. The next day he goes to harvest the second croft; the same thing has happened. That night he takes up his weapons and stands guard over his third field. In the middle of the night, mice swarm into the croft. Each mouse climbs a stalk of wheat, breaks off the ear, and makes away with it. Although Manawydan strikes wildly at the mice, he can't stop them—except for one pudgy, slow mouse, which he manages to catch and imprison in his glove.

The next day, Manawydan takes the mouse up to the top of the Mound of Arberth, and there he builds a little gallows—the mouse is a thief, he tells Cigfa, so he will hang it. One after another, three travelers, each of grander rank than the one before, come by and try to cajole and bribe Manawydan into releasing the mouse. The last of these men finally asks Manawydan what he wants in exchange for the mouse's life. Manawydan demands the return of Rhiannon and Pryderi, the removal of the enchantment from Dyfed, and a guarantee that no further harm will be done to Dyfed or to himself and his family. As Manawydan has correctly divined, this grand traveler is in fact the vengeful magician who has caused all their troubles. But now he accedes to all of Manawydan's conditions; Manawydan and Cigfa are reunited with Rhiannon and Pryderi, and the people, animals, farms, and dwellings of Dyfed reappear, as thriving as ever. And the mouse, set free, is changed back into her true form: the magician's beautiful, very pregnant wife.

The story of Manawydan is full not only of magic, but of humor. This reminds us of the line from the Wiccan Charge of the Goddess: "Let there be mirth and reverence within you." Both can be paths toward knowing the divine. The Charge also states, "Let there be honor and humility," and we see this exemplified, too, in the character of Manawydan. A man of great nobility and honor, he nevertheless does not press his rights when the only reason to do so is pride, nor does he hesitate to work as a humble craftsman when that is the best way to support those who depend on him. He is not even afraid of looking like a fool (building a tiny gallows to hang a mouse!), if that's what will get the job done.

An early Welsh poem says of Manawydan that "he was profound in counsel." His decisions are measured, deliberate, well thought out—"Don't be hasty" might be his motto. He generally seems to decide on the path of least resistance, and may appear overly cautious or too passive. But he has the wisdom and sense of responsibility that come from maturity and experience.

A disastrous war—in which he fought bravely and loyally—has shown him that it is worth seeking alternatives to violence. Very often, insight and intelligence are a far better defense than the sword. In fact, Manawydan's intelligence can be quite wily. He analyzes a situation and then, when the advantage comes within his reach, he seizes it. With his patience, resourcefulness, and creative thinking, "Wait for the opportune moment" could easily be another motto of his!

Manawydan's qualities make him a good friend and ally. Looking closer at his story, we see that he is even more. A man of wisdom, he has been a warrior and becomes a craftsman and then a farmer—so he sums up in himself the principle divisions of Celtic society. He excels at whatever he puts his hands to, and he uses all of his skills for the good of the land and people in his charge. He is, in fact, the type of Celtic deity often referred to as the Chieftain God or God of the Tribe. He is the one to whom the people look to provide for them and the master of all the skills they need to survive and thrive.

Living with Manawydan

One of Manawydan's roles in the Third Branch is as defender of the harvest. This makes any of the autumn harvest festivals a good time to honor him. Planting time, too, is an appropriate occasion to call on Manawydan. Grains and grain products are under his aegis, so it is good to use these in any ritual dedicated to him.

Even if you don't have a farm or a garden, Manawydan's protection of the harvest can still apply to you. All of us depend on food that is grown on farms and in gardens, perhaps in our own neighborhood, perhaps far away in another county, state, or even country. No matter; that food still comes from the labor of people working the earth. We can honor Manawydan by remembering to be thankful for our food and for the work of those who produced it. Moreover, like Manawydan, we are all stewards of the earth, and there are many ways for us to express this: composting, recycling, growing or buying organic produce, and so on. Harvest has another meaning, too, as the result of our labors in whatever field—not just in terms of our job and/or creative endeavors, but in terms of our relationships, our spiritual quests, or what have you. Manawydan can help us with seeing our projects through to completion, and he can help us protect the special things that we have worked for.

The word *work* has come up quite a bit in this discussion of Manawydan, and for good reason. We like to think of him, in one of his aspects, as the god of Right Livelihood. He's a provider, and he's not afraid of hard work. He sees the honor even in humble jobs and does them to the best of his capability. Whether he's functioning as a ruler, an artisan, or a farmer, he's doing what needs to be done, and doing it with the utmost integrity. Obviously, Manawydan is a wonderful god to look to when we are wrestling with issues of work and of earning a living.

Finally, perhaps one of Manawydan's greatest lessons for us lies in his "profoundness in counsel." He reminds us that the voice of experience is worth listening to—and of the value of growing into our own maturity and experience. He cautions us to pay attention to our situation and our surroundings. We should evaluate perceived threats carefully and not jump to conclusions. We should cultivate creative thinking and learn to recognize opportunities for positive action. And here's one more motto for Manawydan and for those who would follow in his footsteps: Learn to choose your battles.

Chapter 16

Lugh and Lleu: Gods of Strength and Skill

The names Lugh (Irish) and Lleu (Welsh), along with Gaulish Lug or Lugos and Romano-Celtic Loucetius or Leucetius, are cognates—words of close form and identical meaning from related languages. These names have to do with light, and, on some level, the deities bearing these names are all gods of light, probably with solar associations, but possibly (or additionally) linked to lightning. The mythology that has come down to us also makes it clear that Lugh and Lleu were gods of skill, strength, and youthful prowess. Yet the tales surrounding these gods are quite different, so that Lugh and Lleu have become known to us as distinct characters.

Lugh

Lugh (the "Shining One") appears on the stage of Irish myth as a radiant, luminous youth who approached the great hall of the Túatha Dé Danann at the Hill of Tara, legendary seat of the high kings of Ireland, when the Túatha Dé were suffering under the oppression of their greatest enemies, the Fomorians. At the time of Lugh's arrival, the king of the Túatha Dé, Nuadu, was presiding over a great feast. The doorkeeper refused to admit Lugh, saying, "No one without an art enters Tara." Trying to reason with the guard, Lugh declared that he was a master carpenter, and thus had a skill to offer. The doorman curtly replied that an accomplished carpenter was already in service to the king. Unabashed, Lugh said that he was a blacksmith, and then a warrior—and then a harper, poet, magician, physician, and so on—only to be told each time that there was already such a person at Tara, and thus his talent was not needed. Finally, Lugh asked if there was any individual in Tara skilled in *all* those arts; at this the doorkeeper consulted with Nuadu, who directed him to let Lugh in. The king, perhaps both amused and unimpressed by Lugh's youthful arrogance, arranged for three tests of Lugh's prowess, involving brute strength, a game of strategy, and the artistry of a bard. Lugh proved himself better than anyone else of the Túatha Dé at each of these challenges. Finally realizing the scope of Lugh's talent, Nuadu not only gave Lugh the epithet of *samildánach*, meaning "skilled in all the crafts," but surrendered his throne to this luminous champion, who set about preparing the Túatha Dé to fight—and defeat—their foes.

Lugh proceeded to rally the gods and heroes of the tribe, asking each one to contribute according to his or her greatest talent. As each member of the Túatha Dé offered his or her distinct gift, it became obvious that the demoralized community actually contained a powerful arsenal of both magical and military powers. Lugh took the first opportunity to provoke the enemy by a blatant act of aggression—killing all but nine of their tax collectors sent to harass the tribe for its annual tribute—thereby setting into motion events that would culminate in a climactic battle, one of the greatest of Irish myth, the second battle of Mag Tuired.

Lugh was no mere hotheaded warrior itching for a fight. Rather, his rapid ascent to power within the Túatha Dé was driven by a prophecy, which stated that he would be the one to deliver the tribe by killing the greatest and most fearsome of the Fomorians, a nearly invincible giant called Balor of the Evil Eye. As it happened, this giant was Lugh's grandfather.

Balor had known of the prophecy since before Lugh's birth, and thus had locked his only daughter, Ethlinn, in a crystal castle on an island in the ocean. Imprisoned there with nine ladies-in-waiting, she was fated to a virginal life under house arrest, thanks to her tyrannical father's need to protect himself. But then Balor (who among other unpleasant qualities was a pirate) raided the Irish coast and brought a magical bull back to his island. The owner of the bull, Cian, son of the Túatha Dé physician Dian Cécht, resolved to raid Balor's island himself and regain his property. With the help of a druidess, Cian disguised himself as a woman and so gained entry into the crystal castle. He promptly seduced not only Ethlinn, but all her ladies-in-waiting as well; then he escaped with his bull, leaving Balor's daughter pregnant. Alas, Balor discovered what had happened, and as Ethlinn gave birth to triplets, he snatched them from her and heaved them into the sea. Two of the babies turned into seals, but the third somehow found his way to shore. That child was Lugh.

Balor was known mostly for his one, huge, evil eye, which could wither away and destroy anything it gazed upon. The Fomorians treated him as a secret weapon; they would position him in battle at a strategic spot and use ropes to open his gargantuan eyelid, which would then devastate everything in its view. At the great battle between the Túatha Dé and the Fomorians, Lugh positioned himself carefully with a slingshot and hurled his ammunition at Balor's great eye, timed to hit it just as the eyelid was peeled back. The force of the shot propelled Balor's eye back through his skull, not only killing him, but leaving the eye gazing backward, destroying a swath of Fomorian warriors.

The destiny of Lugh as the savior of his people forms the heart of his role in Irish myth. But many other stories abound about him. While he was king, his father, Cian, was killed by the sons of his rival, Tuireann. As their punishment, Lugh imposed upon them a terrible price to pay for Cian's honor: traveling about the world, collecting numerous magical tools and treasures. They did all that Lugh asked of them, but, in the process, were mortally wounded. Finally, they appealed to Lugh, who had the power to heal them. But he showed them no compassion, allowing them to die.

Lugh is credited as the creator of one of the four great holidays of the ancient Gael: Lughnasad, which literally means "Lugh's assembly." According to tradition, the god created this harvest festival to commemorate the death of his foster mother Tailtiu; originally, it was said to take place only in the central Irish town where Tailtiu lived, but eventually became a holiday celebrated throughout the land. Lughnasad became a time for games, feats of skill, matchmaking, and the resolution of disputes; in modern times, it has survived as Lammas (a Christian harvest festival) and through a variety of folk customs, such as pilgrimages to mountaintops at places like Croagh Patrick in western Ireland (as a god of light, Lugh appears to have been venerated particularly on hilltops and mountaintops).

Lugh is the ultimate Celtic "golden boy." He does everything correctly, on time, and under budget. He rallied the troops and vanquished the greatest of the enemies—never mind that it was his own grandfather. In other words, Lugh sacrificed even a member of his own family to achieve his goals. He symbolizes pure justice—without mercy. Confident in his own righteousness, he allowed the sons of Tuireann to die, even after they begged him to heal them. What Lugh lacked was an understanding of the spiritual power of mercy and forgiveness—*not* as functions of justice, but as important values in their own right.

Lugh and Brigit

It's interesting to contrast Lugh's qualities and skills with those of Brigit.

Brigit represents the principle of mercy, while Lugh represents the principle of justice. The two could never be lovers; indeed, they probably could not even trust each other! Brigit deals with the Fomorians by marrying one of them and working as long as possible for peace. Lugh, by contrast, provokes them by slaughtering 72 Fomorian tax collectors—who, after all, were only doing their job. Yet spiritually speaking, Lugh and Brigit are balanced one with another: Her day (Imbolc) sits opposite on the Wheel of the Year from Lugh's day. She brings the coming of spring, hope, and new life, while he brings the coming of fruition, harvest, and plenty. Brigit signifies the promise of the future; Lugh represents the results of the present. Both are deities of abundance, but while Brigit represents the need to share (appropriate at the end of winter, when community resources are depleting), Lugh signifies the demand on each person to work for his or her own bounty.

Lugh is a savior figure. He saved his people from the threat of the Fomorians both by rallying and organizing the troops and by single-handedly taking on Balor. Without Lugh, the Túatha Dé might never have defeated their foes, so certainly Lugh is to be honored and revered as a god of protection. And yet, in some ways he is a troubling figure. Did he know he was killing his own grandfather? Ultimately, it doesn't matter. Just as Oedipus was not excused by his ignorance when he killed his father and mated with his mother, so Lugh's killing of his own grandfather reveals the limitations of his goodness, regardless of his knowledge or intent. Lugh represents the kind of single-minded confidence in the rightness of morality and law that would have all murderers summarily executed or all international disputes resolved by the use of force. He may be a god of light, but, without the balancing comfort of darkness, his sheer luminosity threatens to blind us.

Magically speaking, Lugh functions as well as Brigit as a figure of protection. Brigit offers it with a mother's love; Lugh with a father's sense of duty. Lugh will protect us because, in his mind, we are incapable of protecting ourselves. What this means is that Lugh is particularly useful for invoking protection when we are facing forces that are utterly beyond us.

Brigit's protection is more homely, less grand, but less humbling to those she protects. She offers a garden-variety sense of love and hope that can help us face the ordinary demons of doubt; Lugh, meanwhile, represents the "big guns" we must occasionally deploy to destroy the terrifying powers of despair.

Likewise, Brigit and Lugh represent different stages in the process of completing a task, whether mundane or magical. Ask Brigit to bless the beginning of the work, the visionary and planning stage. Then call on Lugh's skill to implement that work and follow it through. Brigit will offer you blessings when you are clueless how to proceed, while Lugh will require that you have a clue, but will then take what you've managed to accomplish on your own and multiply it for truly magical results.

Finally, in Lugh, we see the paradox between the individual and the community. As the master of all skills, Lugh is truly larger than life—no one can live up to his amazing excellence. And yet, he knows how to encourage all the members of a community to pull their resources together, creating a formidable power in their midst. Lugh symbolizes the fact that, in a true community, it is *the community itself* that is "master of all the arts." As individuals offer their abilities to the community, it makes the community stronger—and out of that strength, each member can find protection.

Honoring Lugh

If you wish to honor Lugh in your life, begin by developing your skills. Any skills will do; remember, Lugh is the master of them all. But also hone your sense of law, justice, fair play, and right. Focus particularly on completing your tasks: Lugh is the harvest god, and harvest means completion (no matter what time of year). But especially look to honor Lugh at the beginning of August, the traditional season for Lughnasad. This could be a fun time to engage in playful contests with friends and loved ones, whether intellectual (chess), physical (football), or just plain fun (like Monopoly!).

Lleu

Lleu can be honored in many of the ways that Lugh can. Because of the different emphasis in his mythology, however, many Wiccans who work with Welsh lore prefer to honor him at the solstices and/or equinoxes instead of or in addition to Lughnasad. Meditation on Lleu's story will no doubt yield further ideas for devotional practice.

In Chapter 12, we saw how Lleu Llaw Gyffes was born and how he obtained his name and his arms. His mother then swore that he would never get a wife from among the people now in the world. But his uncle and foster father, Gwydion, was determined that Lleu would have a wife nonetheless. As Patrick K. Ford's translation of the Mabinogi puts it, Lleu now "had a man's physique and was the most handsome fellow anyone ever saw." Gwydion went to his uncle, Math the Ancient, king of Gwynedd in north Wales, a wise magician and teacher. Joining magical forces, they created a woman from the flowers of oak, meadowsweet, and broom. They named her Blodeuedd, "flowers," and she was "the fairest and most beautiful maiden anyone ever saw."

After Lleu married Blodeuedd, Gwydion asked Math to give Lleu territory to rule, and he received the part of Gwynedd known as Ardudwy. He ruled well, so that all the people were pleased with him. After a time, he went away to visit Math. While he was gone, a nobleman on a stag hunt, Gronw the Strong, came by Lleu's court. As was proper, Blodeuedd offered him hospitality. As they feasted and talked, they fell in love. Gronw stayed three days and nights with Blodeuedd, who was happy for his company and his love. Gronw made certain to leave before Lleu returned, but not without first persuading Blodeuedd to find out how her husband could be killed so that she could be with Gronw instead.

Lleu came home, and when he and Blodeuedd were in bed together, she told him she was worried he might die and leave her alone. He reassured her by telling her how unlikely the conditions of his death were: Only a spear crafted for a year and a day during sacred time could kill him, and then only if he was neither in a house nor outside and neither on a horse nor on foot. And then he told her exactly how these conditions could be brought about.

She sent word to Gronw, and a year and a day later the spear was ready. Blodeuedd arranged for a tub to be set up under a roof frame on the bank of the Cynfael River, facing the water and with the hill Bryn Cyfergyr rising behind it. Lleu went there to bathe, and, when he was done, Blodeuedd stationed a billy goat beside the tub. Lleu climbed out, one foot on the edge of the tub, one on the billy goat's back. At that moment, Gronw, waiting on Bryn Cyfergyr, stood and cast his spear. It struck Lleu in the side. He cried out, and his cry became that of a bird. Transformed into a golden eagle, he flew away out of sight.

Sometime later, Gwydion found him perched at the top of an oak tree and restored him to human form. After nearly a year spent healing, Lleu was ready to seek justice for his wrongs. He and Gwydion mustered the forces of Math and led them to Ardudwy. Blodeuedd and her maidens tried to escape by fleeing the court and climbing a mountain. The maidens fell, one by one, into the lake below; meanwhile, Gwydion turned Blodeuedd into an owl. Gronw offered Lleu money and lands, but Lleu demanded that Gronw go to the bank of the Cynfael and stand where Lleu had stood, while Lleu would be on Bryn Cyfergyr and would cast a spear at him. He allowed Gronw, however, to place a stone between the two of them. Then Lleu cast the spear so strongly that it pierced the stone and Gronw alike. Gronw died, and Lleu took possession of his land again. He ruled well, and later, "according to the lore," was lord over all of Gwynedd.

Light and Darkness

We are fortunate that the Fourth Branch preserves so much lore about Lleu Llaw Gyffes, and yet it is clear that much more existed in the past. The Triads call him one of the Three Red Ravagers of the Island of Britain—a compliment to his skill in battle. Medieval Welsh poetry contains references to Lleu, in company with Gwydion, as an accomplished enchanter and bard. Lleu, like Lugh, is a warrior skilled in many arts! Lleu also appears at Gwydion's side in some versions of "Cad Goddeu" ("The Battle of the Trees"). In addition, this poem contains a passage describing the creation of Blodeuedd.

Lleu's marriage is one of the most significant features of his distinctive mythic identity. On the surface, Arianrhod's declaration that he will never have a wife from among the people now in this world is nothing but a spiteful curse. Looking deeper, we can see other possible interpretations. One, for example, is that because he is a divine child, he must have a divine bride. Another view is that because he will be a ruler, he must marry the land itself—and Blodeuedd, made from plants and flowers, is the walking spirit of the land. The birds associated with them also symbolize the balance between them: he is the eagle, the great daylight hunter; she is the owl, the hunter in the night.

Lleu has a strong connection with another bird, too: the wren. (Remember, it was by striking a wren that he earned his name.) In both Ireland and Wales, the wren is known as the king of birds, and an old Welsh folktale tells why: The birds had a contest to see who could fly highest, and that bird would be their king. The eagle soared up and up, not realizing that a clever little wren was hitchhiking on his back. When the eagle was exhausted and could go no higher, the wren took off and flew above him, thus winning the kingship of the birds. In other parts of Britain, there is a tradition that the wren alternates his rule with that of the robin: The wren rules from Midsummer (Summer Solstice) to Midwinter (Winter Solstice), and the robin the other half of the year.

Lleu's story makes careful note of the passage of time in the crafting of the spear that kills him and then in his subsequent healing. This, combined with the wren motif, suggests that one way of understanding him is as a god who in a sense embodies the Wheel of the Year, the never-ending cycle of birth, growth, decay, death, and rebirth. This is seen in plant and animal life, and is echoed by the apparent growth and diminishing of the sun as the hours of daylight lengthen till Midsummer then diminish till Midwinter. It is worth remembering that, in the British Isles, daylight lasts for a very long time indeed at the Summer Solstice, while there is so little daylight at the Winter Solstice that it can seem as though the sun has all but died.

In the Fourth Branch of the Mabinogi, one of Lleu's most important aspects is as a dying-and-rising god. Moreover, he reveals the conditions of his death willingly—and, we can assume, knowing full well what is coming. For the wheel of life to continue turning as it should, he knows that he must embrace death, and makes of himself a willing sacrifice. He shows us, however, that death is simply transformation: The divine light takes many forms, but can never be extinguished.

Chapter 17

Oenghus: The Young Lover

Many of the Celtic deities (such as Macha, Cú Chulainn, and the Morrígan) are renowned as fearsome warriors—who may be gifted at battle or headhunting, but somehow seem to lack the kind of finesse necessary to, say, nurse a sick child. Lugh displays mastery of all skills, and the Dagda combines his prowess in battle with a coarse sense of humor—but these multitalented deities could give the impression that Celtic myth is, mostly, a celebration of aggression.

For this reason, the Irish god known as Oenghus, or Angus Óg ("Angus the Young") is an important reminder of the depth and texture in Celtic mythology. He is also called Angus mac Óg, or Angus the Young Son. One of his epithets is Angus of the Birds—hardly the kind of title a mighty warrior would proudly wear! True enough, Oenghus is important not for his military prowess or physical might, but for being a different kind of champion—in the service of love.

Youth is the key to understanding this most delicate of the gods. Celtic lore points out that he went from conception to birth in a single day (which may not be quite as remarkable as it sounds: Oenghus was born out of wedlock to the Dagda and Boann, and his parents magically caused the day on which he was conceived to last for nine months so that Boann could give birth to her love child without her husband ever being the wiser). After his birth, the young god was fostered to a fairy lord, Midhir. Combining his mother's beauty with his father's exuberant charm, Oenghus developed a reputation as the god who aided lovers in need. He makes his home at the magical site known today as Newgrange, the 5,000-year-old passage tomb that is easily Ireland's most famous prehistoric monument. To the ancients, it was Brugh na Bóinne, "the hostel on the Boyne River."

Set in a lush, fertile valley of verdant farmland, with the river that bears his mother's name gliding lazily by, Oenghus's mythical home seems befitting for the god of love. Tradition holds that when Oenghus lived at Brugh na Bóinne, the trees were always heavily laden with fruit and a cooked pig was always ready for feasting. It was the ultimate in hospitality, for Oenghus embodied love in all its forms—not only the passion of romance, but the good cheer of friendship as well. An interesting link to his mother (whose name suggests that before she became the goddess of the Boyne River, Boann was a cow goddess) is found in one legend that Oenghus worked with the sea god Manannán mac Lir to bring the first cows to Ireland.

To Whom Lovers Turn

As the patron of love, Oenghus appears more than once in Irish myth as a figure to whom lovers in need would turn for assistance. One of the most famous of Oenghus's protégés is Diarmaid, the young god's foster son who was given a *ball seirce* ("love spot") or beauty mark by a fairy lover, which made him irresistible to women. This might sound like a handy blemish to have, but it unfortunately led to a disastrous love affair when Diarmaid became embroiled in a romantic triangle with the lovely Gráinne, who was betrothed to marry Diarmaid's captain, Finn mac Cumhaill. She abandoned her fiancé the moment Diarmaid's beauty spot worked its magic on her. Even Oenghus could not prevent this affair from ending tragically.

Another tale involving the young god of love is even more tragic: the story of fair Étain, a hapless woman who is seduced by Oenghus's foster father, Midhir. Alas, Midhir's first wife, Fuamnach, reacts with jealous hostility to her husband's new lover, turning Étain into a butterfly and causing a magical wind to blow her far away. Oenghus provides shelter for the butterfly-maiden until an opportunity comes for her to be swallowed by a mortal woman, who then becomes pregnant and gives birth to Étain reincarnated, according to legend, over 1,000 years after she first lived in human form! By this time, the Irish gods have surrendered the land to the Celts and have retired to life underground in the fairy mounds. The reborn Étain, fairest woman in Ireland, grows up to marry the high king, only to have the persistent Midhir engage in all sorts of trickery to regain her.

The story, which comes down to us in fragmentary form, offers little hope for a truly happy ending.

The Dream of Cáer

If it's beginning to seem that Oenghus's abilities as a god of love may be lacking, consider the most famous story involving him, in which Oenghus himself is smitten by romance.

He has a dream of a woman so lovely that he becomes heartsick with desire for her; he knows she is real, but the dream leaves him with no knowledge of who his nocturnal lover might be. He wastes away with longing for her, but also resolves to find her, and searches throughout Ireland for an entire year, but in vain. Concerned for Oenghus's health, the Dagda and others help him in his quest. Finally, with the assistance of King Ailill of Connacht, he learns that the woman of his dreams (literally) is named Cáer Ibormeith ("Yew Berry") and lives with her 150 companions on a lake. As it turns out, Cáer is a shapeshifter, and spends alternating years as a human and as a swan.

When he appeals to her father, Oenghus discovers that the only way to win Cáer's love is to woo her while she is in swan form. Her shapeshifting occurs each year at the festival of Samhain (the end of summer), so the young god waits until that time and then goes to the lake to approach her. Challenged by the fact that all of Cáer's companions have likewise transformed into swans, Oenghus nonetheless finds his lover among the birds, and turns himself into a swan so that he might court her as an equal. At last united, the two swans take flight from the lake, heading for Brugh na Bóinne; as they circle above the lake three times, they begin to sing—a love song of such Otherworldly beauty that anyone who hears it is lulled to a restful sleep that lasts for three days.

The Ambiguity of Love

Between the warlike energies found in so much Celtic myth and the sadness that permeates many a Celtic love tale, how does an ambiguous love god like Oenghus speak to us today? Perhaps the first point to consider when meditating on Oenghus is his willingness to help lovers, even if their motivations or goals are not the most noble. Love strikes the human heart in many circumstances and settings, and all too often it seems that jealousy, infidelity, broken engagements, or manipulative trickery persist as love's unflagging companions. Oenghus passes no moral judgment—he simply helps love to grow, leaving it up to us to make the sometimes difficult choices when the love we feel may not be what is truly for the best. Indeed, stories like those of Diarmaid and Gráinne or Midhir and Étain serve as stark reminders of how the power of love can be as much a force for terrible destruction as it is a force for life and joy.

Still, the message here is not just a bleak warning—Oenghus's own dramatic entry into the world of love ends lyrically and happily. The young god never ceases in his yearlong quest to find his dream beloved, and refuses even to let Cáer's shapeshifting stand between the union of their hearts. When it comes time to make a final decision, Oenghus does what any true lover would: He dives deep into his passion and transforms *himself*, taking what others might have seen as an obstacle and instead creates a powerful and inspiring declaration of love. Finally, they sealed their shared destiny by joining together in a song of Otherworldly beauty (that induced sleep to those who heard it). One can only wonder how many people, sleeping for three days after hearing Cáer and Oenghus's celestial melody, dreamt of their own true love.

For honoring Oenghus today, naturally he is the go-to god concerning all matters of the heart. Unfortunately, he is not one to provide useful advice on love—better stick with a more discerning deity such as Arianrhod or Manannán for guidance as to whether your choices in love are truly in alignment with your highest good. Call on Oenghus only when you are confident beyond any doubt that the romance you hold is truly your soul's deepest love. Oenghus will bless your love, shelter those who suffer, and assist in the removal of obstacles—but he takes no responsibility for any chaos or mayhem that may ensue.

This is especially important to bear in mind when considering using magic in the pursuit of love. Spells cast to win a specific person's love are almost always problematic: Any attempt to manipulate another person's free will, magical or otherwise, is unethical and spiritually dangerous. For this reason, all ethical teachers insist that any magical work done in the interest of love be done strictly on one's own self. In other words, don't cast a spell to make person X fall in love with you; instead, work your magic to increase your own natural ability to love and your own natural attractiveness so that the right person (whoever that may be) will be more likely to freely notice you and make the connection.

For the time of year best suited to honoring Oenghus, consider Samhain, because that was the time when he and Cáer were finally united. But given Samhain's overall themes of death and release, it is not always a holiday one would devote to the lighter energies of youth and romance. Therefore, many devotees of Oenghus prefer to venerate him in the spring—either Imbolc or Beltaine, or the Spring Equinox. Imbolc is particularly appropriate because of the traditions linking Oenghus to Brigit (see Chapter 6). Even the Summer Solstice (a time of year typically favored for weddings) can be a wonderful holiday for seeking a closer connection to the patron of love. After all, love never goes out of style!

Finally, a literary note: Oenghus is immortalized in William Butler Yeats' gorgeous poem, "The Song of Wandering Aengus," recounting the perseverance of a lover who has glimpsed, but not attained, his soul mate. Filled with romantic and mystical imagery, it is a shimmering lyric not only of human love, but equally of the love a mortal might feel for the goddess he adores.

Chapter 18

Cú Chulainn:
The Hound of Ulster

Cú Chulainn is the greatest hero of legendary Ireland. A semi-divine figure whose father was the god Lugh, he is the warrior par excellence in the Irish tradition—arguably the greatest warrior of *all* Celtic lore. He is a champion whose inspiration as a national hero lives on in the Emerald Isle today, and whose larger-than-life exploits both on and off the battlefield have helped to give Celtic mythology its grandeur and excitement. Brigit may be the personification of beauty, Cernunnos the epitome of wildness, and Rhiannon the height of grace—but with Cú Chulainn, you get nonstop, heart-pounding action. He'd make a great leading character in a modern Hollywood testosterone-drenched blockbuster—with lots of blood and guts and gore, of course.

This ultimate warrior is the star of the second of the four great Irish mythic cycles, known as the Ulster Cycle because most of the action takes place in the northern province. He is the major figure in the great Irish national epic, *Táin Bó Cuailnge* ("The Cattle Raid of Cooley"), in which his most formidable adversary is the treacherous Queen Medb. His status as a semi-divine hero comes from being the child of a mortal mother, Deichtine, who was impregnated by Lugh, the radiant god of skill, justice, and triumph in battle—a fitting father to this unstoppable war machine. The tradition includes a variety of stories offering differing accounts of how he was born; in one tale Deichtine drinks water that contains the presence of Lugh, while another tale has Lugh coming to her in a dream. The stories of his birth tend to stress her virginity, perhaps thereby strengthening Cú Chulainn's claim to be semi-divine—and putting him squarely in the worldwide tradition of the mythological hero, who across many cultures is often born of a virgin mother and a royal or divine father (indeed, some stories of his birth suggest his father was not Lugh, but rather Conchobar, the king of Ulster in whose court the hero would eventually serve).

The Boyhood Deeds

Deichtine names the boy Sétanta (which means "the knower of ways") and fosters him to the king of Ulster, the aforementioned Conchobar (who may have been Deichtine's brother and therefore Sétanta's uncle). Some traditions suggest that the boy had seven foster fathers, who provided for him in a variety of ways, not only by providing material comfort, but also by giving him training in poetry, eloquence, and other skills. Numerous tales stress the young hero's marvelous boyhood deeds, including defeating 150 other boys in combat and vanquishing an attack of demons that threaten Emain Macha (the royal site of Ulster, named for the great goddess Macha).

When Sétanta was 7 years old, he was late to a feast being held by the smith Culann, and arrived outside the feast hall to find the smith's hound guarding the door. The hound was gigantic and dangerously ferocious. Even as a boy, Sétanta possessed heroic abilities, so when the dog attacked him, he promptly killed the beast. Although the boy was unharmed, this was distressing to Culann, whose guard dog was now dead. The 7-year-old gallantly offered to raise another hound and train it to be Culann's guard dog; while the puppy was growing, Sétanta himself would serve as Culann's "hound." This was how he got his adult name—Cú Chulainn means "hound of Culann"—and may also be the source of his most important *geis*, or sacred injunction, never to eat the flesh of a dog.

Not long after taking his adult name, the boy overheard a druid prophecy that, on a certain day, whoever took up arms would live a short but glorious life. Resolved that such renown meant more to him than longevity, Cú Chulainn went straight to the king and asked to take up arms that day. The king agreed, but all the weapons presented to the boy were too fragile for him to handle; in the end, only the king's own arms were sturdy enough for the young hero.

Overflowing with raw masculinity as he was, Cú Chulainn, not surprisingly, was said to be quite attractive to women. But befitting his semidivine nature, he was often described in many supernatural ways: he had seven fingers and seven toes, seven pupils in each eye, a hawk's grip in his hand, four dimples in each cheek (colored red, yellow, blue, and green), and three different colors to his hair (brown, blood-red, and blond).

Cú Chulainn chose Emer to be his wife; but she was no pushover and insisted that only a worthy man might marry her. Her father established a series of near-impossible tasks for the boy to complete before he could gain Emer's hand. He was required to receive training from a woman warrior named Scáthach, who lived on an island in the Hebrides. He performed a variety of feats as part of this training, including seducing both Scáthach and her daughter, Uathach, as well as Scáthach's rival Aífe! Eventually, he had to defeat Emer's father and his men before he could claim her as his bride. Although Cú Chulainn was said to have had a number of lovers, Emer was always seen as his first or main wife.

While striving to win Emer's hand, Cú Chulainn fought and killed three hostile warriors known as the Sons of Nechtan. During this battle, he experienced the terrifying shift in both his consciousness and physical appearance called the *riastradh*—the "battle frenzy" or "warp-spasm." The description of the *riastradh* is graphic and astounding: Cú Chulainn's body twisted about within his skin; his lips peeled back from his mouth revealing the bone around his teeth, so much so that his quivering heart and liver were visible through his jaws; one eye sank deep within his skull while the other fell out of its socket, dangling by his cheek. His heart boomed as loud as a kettledrum, and a spout of blood gushed geyserlike from a hole in the crown of his head.

It's a description of the adrenaline of rage as befits the extra-large dimensions of Celtic myth (and the Cú Chulainn legend in particular). Once in this state, the Hound of Ulster could kill 40 with a single blow. Apparently the warp-spasm was so dangerous that, once he entered it, no one was safe—not even friends or comrades. One time when Cú Chulainn is seen approaching Emain Macha in the *riastradh*, the alarmed king sent the women of Ulster out to greet him—naked. Apparently that was what it took to shock him (or shame him, or perhaps even turn him on) enough so that, distracted, he could be grabbed by the Ulstermen—but still his rage continued, and they had to dump him into three vats of cold water (the first of which exploded, the second of which boiled over) before he finally snapped out of his lethal altered state.

For all his boyhood exploits, Cú Chulainn was destined to encounter tragedy through another boy—his own son by Aífe, named Connla. The boy is under a *geis* never to reveal his name. When at age 7 he travels to Ireland to join his father, he defeats any man who stands in his way. Soon enough, Cú Chulainn is called to challenge this mysterious boy who is advancing on Emain Macha. The two do combat, and without realizing what he is doing, the father kills his own son.

A Living War Machine

More than once in his short life, Cú Chulainn embodied his arche-typal role as a hero when he was called to defend his province single-handedly. During the great cattle raid of Cooley, for example, he was required to face Medb's army alone, for all of his Ulster companions fell under the curse of Macha, which left them debilitated with the pains that women in labor experience (see Chapter 9). This curse became manifest only at the time of Ulster's greatest need—certainly typified by the threat posed by the queen of Connacht's army. Various stories recount Cú Chulainn's prowess in battle. Perhaps the most poignant moment in the *Táin* came when he had to face, and kill, his best friend, who fought for Medb.

Eventually, the Morrígán noticed him, and she came to him as an earthly princess, seeking his love. When he rudely rebuffed her, she re-vealed her true identity and swore to be his enemy. From then on, she harried him in a variety of shapeshifting forms: as an eel, a heifer, and a wolf. After he wounded her, she appeared to him as an old beggar woman who offered him milk from her cow, thereby tricking him into blessing her. Toward the end of his life, she may have been the crone who offered him stew made of dog's meat, thereby creating a mortal dilemma—for he had a *geis* never to refuse hospitality that was as serious as his *geis* against eating dog flesh. He accepted the stew and ate it, thereby setting into motion the events that would culminate in his death.

Other accounts point to Medb as the architect of Cú Chulainn's de-mise. She joined forces with three sorceresses, who sought revenge against the hero for killing their father; they fashioned three enchanted spears, each of which was said to be fated to kill a king. The spears were carried into battle by foes of Cú Chulainn. The first one was thrown at the Hound of Ulster but killed his charioteer, "the king of charioteers;" the second one killed his horse, the Gray of Macha, "the king of horses;" and, finally, the third spear mortally wounded Cú Chulainn himself, "the king of warriors."

Near death, with his bowels spilling out of the horrendous wound from the cursed spear, Cú Chulainn strapped his badly wounded body to a standing stone, perhaps to die on his feet, perhaps to keep fighting to the last. Different stories depict his end in various ways: In one tradition, war-riors feared to come near him until the Morrígán, as a raven, landed on his shoulder; in one tale, a warrior finally beheaded him, only to have the dead hero's arm fall, still holding his sword, severing a limb from his vanquisher.

Even in death, the greatest Irish hero must strike the last blow. But dead he was—and only 27 years old.

The Legacy of Cú Chulainn

Unlike many figures of Celtic mythology who are known to us only in fragmentary or mysterious ways, Cú Chulainn is a figure of whom many stories are told, and who has continued to be lionized in poem, prose, song, and art into our own time. As was mentioned in Chapter 7, a famous statue stands in the General Post Office of Dublin, depicting the young warrior in death; it commemorates those who died in that post office in the spring of 1916 during an uprising on the eve of the Irish war for independence.

But when we take the time to listen carefully to the soul of the Cú Chulainn myth, beneath the warp-spasm and tall-tale talk, what emerges is a profound glimpse at the frightening power of human rage, a power that in its own way seems as explosive—and deadly—as anything unleashed at Hiroshima or Nagasaki. Cú Chulainn is a mythic sign for us, in which we recognize that the peak emotional experiences of the frenzied warrior are world-shattering in their intensity. After all, the Hound of Ulster was no mere warrior; as he approached battle he became a killing monster of gargantuan proportions.

So what is the spiritual lesson here? Perhaps it's related to Theodore Roosevelt's advice: "Speak softly and carry a big stick." A warrior achieves nothing by being only somewhat frightening. And while in our post-nuclear world it's often difficult to integrate the spirit of a warrior with the path of inner wisdom, in truth we cannot be peacemakers without also being capable of defending our boundaries and fighting for what is right (even if what is right is working for a world beyond war).

Shapeshifting is a nearly universal magical skill, and Cú Chulainn's warp-spasm is about as shifted as a shape can get. But rage is not the only gateway to an altered state. We can find transformative spiritual power in the ecstasy of enlightenment as easily as in the rage of conflict. And in the end, what makes Cú Chulainn finally a tragic figure is that he proves incapable of anything beyond his frenzies. For this warrior demigod, the warp-spasm is his *only* path to heightened consciousness.

Some clever soul once said, "When the only tool you have is a hammer, every problem starts looking like a nail." And so it is with Cú Chulainn: He kills his own son, his own best friend, and very nearly every able-bodied man in Ireland, all because that's the limit of his skill. Unlike his many-skilled father, the greatest of heroes has but one talent: to kill. Granted, this he does well. But at the end of the great cattle raid, he fails to protect the brown bull of Cooley. He fails to be a father to his only child.

Perhaps most important for us, he fails to recognize the goddess (the Morrigán) when she approaches him. On another occasion (when a vulnerable Medb begs for mercy), he can only relate to the feminine energy with contempt. The Morrigán and Medb do not forget the sting of his rejection, and so it is they, more than anyone else, who see to it that he doesn't live for his 30th birthday. Obsessed with the idolatry of his own violent ideals, Cú Chulainn rejects the feminine—the goddess—as weak. And in so doing, he exposes his own weakness, to his final defeat.

For the 21st-century seeker of Celtic wisdom, few mythic figures are as important as Lugh's son. Cú Chulainn reminds us of all that is great and noble about the warrior's ideal—and likewise stands as a somber warning of the consequences of that ideal taken to an out-of-balance extreme. Certainly we honor this hero whenever we take a stand, or fight for what's right, or push ourselves to achieve results beyond what anyone thought possible. Yet, in its own curious way, the spirituality of Ulster's Hound is also honored when we *lay down* our weapons, or when we choose to make love, not war. If you have difficulties with rage or violence, learn to control those impulses. If you have a child being raised far away, get involved in his or her life, before it's too late. And if the goddess should come to you, offer her hospitality; no matter how busy or angry or engaged in battle you may be, do not reject her. In this, you will revere Cú Chulainn far more than mere prowess in battle ever could.

The best time of year for honoring this great and tragic figure would probably be while the days are getting shorter—Lughnasad (a day sacred to Cú Chulainn's father) or Samhain would be particularly appropriate festivals to venerate Ulster's finest son. Likewise, the Winter Solstice could be a day for symbolically releasing the violence-blind warrior, thereby creating room for the "rebirth" of the "sun"—calling back into Cú Chulainn's mythic life the many skills and keen sense of justice embodied by his father.

Cú Chulainn helps us to see the naked, raw power inherent in taking something as far as it will go. He also reminds us that the line that separates "pushing against the limits" from "going over the edge" is thin indeed. When you choose to work with this figure's energy, be mindful of that line—always. It is more essential than you could ever know, short of pushing beyond it. And then paying the consequences.

Chapter 19

Gwydion:
The Trickster-Magician

We have encountered Gwydion mab Dôn already in some of his interactions with Arianrhod (his sister) and Lleu Llaw Gyffes (his nephew and foster son). These events take place in the second half of the Fourth Branch of the Mabinogi. The first part of that Branch introduces Gwydion at the court of his uncle, Math the Ancient, king of Gwynedd. One day, Gwydion comes upon his brother Gilfaethwy looking very mopey and ill because of his unfulfilled yearning for Goewin, Math's virgin footholder. The maiden is always with Math, so Gilfaethwy cannot get her alone. Gwydion decides to help his brother out by starting a war, because only while leading his army can Math be away from his footholder.

First, Gwydion goes to Math and tells him that Pryderi, the king of Dyfed in the south, has got a new kind of animal called swine or pigs, "whose meat is better than beef." These were a gift to Pryderi from Arawn, the ruler of Annwn (in Celtic lore, domestic animals are often portrayed as gifts of the Otherworld). Naturally, Math would like to have pigs for his realm, too, so he gives Gwydion permission to try to obtain some.

Gwydion disguises himself and 11 companions as poets, and they set off for Pryderi's court, where they are, of course, welcomed. "Then," as Patrick K. Ford puts it in his translation of the Mabinogi, "Gwydion was the best reciter of lore in the world. That night he entertained the court with pleasing monologues and lore that was admired by everyone of the court, and Pryderi found it delightful to be entertained by him."

Gwydion takes advantage of this kind reception and asks Pryderi out-right for the pigs from Annwn. Pryderi, however, has given his word to Arawn that he will not let anyone else have the pigs until they have doubled their number in Dyfed. Gwydion finds a way around this: "Don't *give* them to me then," he says. "Tomorrow I'll bring you something to *trade* for them." So during the night, he uses his magic to conjure 12 horses with 12 splendid saddles and bridles, 12 hunting dogs with 12 leashes and collars that look as if they are made of gold, and 12 golden shields. The next morning, he offers all of these to Pryderi in exchange for the swine, and the bargain is successfully concluded.

Gwydion and his men immediately start to herd the pigs north, mov-ing as swiftly as possible since the enchantment will only last for a day. Sure enough, back at Pryderi's court the golden shields turn back into mushrooms; likewise, the horses, hounds, and all the splendid trappings revert to the materials from which Gwydion conjured them. By the time Gwydion and the swine reach Math's territory, Pryderi and his army are in pursuit of the pig rustler. All is going according to Gwydion's plan!

Math heads out to the battlefield, as do Gwydion and Gilfaethwy. But at night, the two brothers sneak back to the fortress. They go straight to Math's bedchamber, forcing the handmaids out, and Gilfaethwy gets into bed with Goewin. "The girl was seduced dishonorably," says the Mabinogi, "and slept with against her will that night."

Gwydion and Gilfaethwy get back to the battle in the morning. After two or three disastrous encounters in which many men are killed on each side, Pryderi offers to meet Gwydion in single combat, lest more men die because of the quarrel between the two of them. With every appearance of honor, Gwydion agrees. But during the combat, he uses magic to gain the upper hand, and kills Pryderi.

He doesn't enjoy his victory for long. As soon as Math returns to his fortress, Goewin tells him how she was raped. Math's first action is to do what is in his power to make things right with Goewin: He marries her and puts his realm in her hands. Then he outlaws his two nephews, who have not returned to court. Finally, after a time of foraging through the countryside, Gwydion and Gilfaethwy come before Math to accept pun-ishment for their deeds.

Math takes up his staff of enchantment and strikes each man, turning Gwydion into a stag and Gilfaethwy into a doe. Then he sends them away to live as animals and mate with each other. After a year, they return with a fawn, whom Math takes from them. Now he turns Gwydion into a wild sow and Gilfaethwy into a wild boar, again sending them into the wilderness. A year later, they return with their piglet. Finally, Math transforms Gwydion into a wolf and Gilfaethwy into a wolf bitch. At the end of the year, they bring Math their pup.

Math takes the brothers' three offspring and transforms them into strong little boys, who grow up to be famous warriors. Then, at last, he returns Gwydion and Gilfaethwy to their human forms. After they are bathed and properly clothed, he pronounces their punishment complete. All that remains is for Gwydion to recommend a new footholder—as we saw in Chapter 12.

"When the Trees Were Enchanted"

Gwydion's other major mythological appearance is in the Battle of the Trees (Cad Goddeu), which is referred to in various pieces of poetry and prose. This was a battle in which Gwydion enchanted trees and other plants to help him, his brother Amaethon ("plowman" or "farmer"), and Lleu fight against the forces of Annwn. Triad 84 calls it one of the Three Futile Battles of the Island of Britain; it was fought over a dog, a roebuck, and a plover or lapwing. Another source says that Amaethon caught a white roebuck and a greyhound pup that came from Annwn, and that this was the reason for the battle. In either case, what we see is three archetypes of Celtic society—the warrior (Lleu), the farmer (Amaethon), and the man of learning (Gwydion)—striving to bring back the gifts of the Otherworld and fighting to keep them. (We would not be surprised if some lost version of the myth also included Gofannon, the archetypal craftsman, as part of this enterprise.)

In one source, the champion of Annwn can only be defeated if his name is known—and Gwydion discerns this by identifying the alder tree depicted in the warrior's crest: "Brân you are, by the branch you bear." Gwydion has the upper hand at Cad Goddeu because of his knowledge of the natural world and his magical ability to bring in the trees on his side. Indeed, much of his magic is based in nature: He enchants mushrooms, leaves, seaweed, trees, etc. One could say he manipulates nature to gain his own ends. It is equally possible, especially as he grows in wisdom, that he is able to work this magic because he understands that all things have the same inner essence, which can take any form or appearance. He is a master at altering the illusions that we call "reality."

Throughout Welsh tradition, Gwydion is renowned as the wizard or magician par excellence. In fact, his name probably means something like "Great Wizard."[1] The Welsh word for *wizard* also seems to connect to one of the words for *wood*, and is close to one that means *wild*. We may read this as an indication that in Pagan Britain, untamed nature was a prime source of magical power. Another essential component of Celtic wizardry appears to have been experiential knowledge, as we can see when we look at the modern Welsh word *gwyddon*, which means both "wizard" and "scientist."

From Selfishness to Sacrifice

In the early part of the Fourth Branch, Gwydion provides a real object lesson on the misuse of power and the squandering of one's gifts. He uses his magic, his cleverness, and his closeness to the throne to start a war, apparently for the main purpose of setting up a rape. He misleads his uncle and sovereign, steals the wealth of another kingdom, and deceives and kills an honorable lord. Along the way, he does introduce a valuable new kind of livestock into his homeland—but at high cost and with reckless disregard for others. He is full of hubris, believing that his knowledge and his talents exempt him from any kind of moral restraint. How are we to honor such a god?

Some women find it particularly difficult to work with Gwydion because of his participation in the rape of Goewin. It is a challenge to find a deep spiritual meaning within that action. Gwydion's story, however, is encouraging in some ways. In the myth, his transgression is recognized as very serious indeed, and he receives a punishment that fits the crime. His own will, voice, and power over his body are taken away from him for three years, during which he must live in a succession of animal forms. One of his animal incarnations is as a female, and he undergoes mating, pregnancy, and birth. When his human form is at last returned to him, his understanding and compassion are far larger than before. His cleverness-for-its-own-sake is beginning to give way to wisdom.

Then, when he undertakes raising Lleu Llaw Gyffes as his own son, he once and for all leaves behind his former hubris and selfishness. Faced with the demands of fatherhood, he realizes that he is not, as he'd once thought, the center of the universe. In placing the needs of his foster son foremost, even above his own desires, he learns the meaning of sacrifice. He sees that all his knowledge is empty (and even dangerous) without love and wisdom to guide it. He is not the same person, but a man redeemed—and he shows that redemption is possible for anyone.

It can be argued that Gwydion's truest act of magic is his finding of the long-missing, wounded Lleu in his eagle form. In Chapter 11 we saw that Gwydion hunted in vain for Lleu until he spent a night in a peasant's house. When he heard that the family had a sow who was behaving oddly, he instantly discerned a connection between the animal and his missing foster son. As Alwyn Rees and Brinley Rees write in *Celtic Heritage* (p. 347), "The discovery of points where unrelated things coincide is one of the great arts of seers and magicians."

Gwydion's magic doesn't stop there. Seeing the eagle in the topmost branches of the tree, he sings a stanza of poetry, which coaxes the eagle into the middle branches. A second stanza brings the eagle to the lowest branch, and the third brings him into Gwydion's lap. Then, with a touch of his magician's staff, Gwydion restores Lleu to his human form, and carries him home to be healed.

This is magic indeed. It is motivated by love; informed equally by knowledge and wisdom; powered by a focused, well-trained will; and carried out by means of words whose potency is increased by their poetic form and their sung utterance. This magic sees beneath appearances and recognizes possibilities. It is a change of consciousness that changes the world.

Living with Gwydion

Mythological characters often transgress the rules of normal human society—and when they make mistakes, they make them on a grand scale. Hopefully, our mistakes are not so dire in their scope and consequences. But when we do something wrong, realize that we have done so, and desire to do better, Gwydion is a deity we might turn to—one who understands accepting consequences and then learning from one's failures. In this process, a dose of humility can be an excellent antidote to the hubris that may have led us into trouble in the first place.

One of Gwydion's major aspects—one often overlooked—is as a father. When Gwydion takes on the responsibility of raising his nephew, he does it wholeheartedly. He teaches Lleu and looks to his needs, physical and emotional, short-term and long-term. When Lleu has difficulties, Gwydion uses all his own skill and ingenuity to help the boy surmount them. When even he cannot shield Lleu from the harsher realities of life, he grieves. But no matter what, Gwydion is always there for his foster son. In fact, it is as a father that Gwydion is at his most appealing, and he is a god to whom any loving father can turn for support.

Gwydion is also a god of knowledge and its pursuit, especially in the natural sciences. At the same time, he was renowned as a poet, storyteller, and "reciter of lore"—so literature, history, genealogy, and similar areas of study could fall under his aegis as well. In fact, few figures in Celtic mythology are equal to him in the use of words, poetically, magically, and persuasively. So this is another thing that Gwydion reminds us of: to cultivate our powers of speech, and also to watch how we use our words. Do we employ them selfishly, twisting them to deceive or mislead others (as Gwydion does in the early part of the Fourth Branch)? Or do our words, coming from a place of love and a desire for harmony, turn to healing, to connecting with others, to increasing wisdom? Words have power. And with power comes responsibility—that is one of the lessons of Gwydion that we should try to carry with us every day.

Chapter 20

Brân:
Guardian of the Land

The Second Branch of the Mabinogi tells the story of the children of Llyr, and in particular of Brân and Branwen. Brân was king of Britain, the Isle of the Mighty. To make an alliance with him, the king of Ireland, Matholwch, sought Branwen in marriage. All of her brothers agreed except for Efnisien, who was away traveling. Finding out about the marriage on his return, he took offense and mutilated Matholwch's horses. To make reparation, Brân gave Matholwch a great treasure, the Cauldron of Rebirth. This cauldron had the power to reanimate the dead—who would not, however, regain their ability to speak.

Matholwch sailed back to Ireland with Branwen, who was at first held in honor at the Irish court, especially after she bore a son, Gwern ("alder"). But then some of the king's men began whispering against her and her brothers, saying that the king had not been sufficiently recompensed for his injured horses. As a result, Matholwch struck Branwen and banished her to the kitchens. Then he banned commerce between Ireland and Wales and imprisoned any Welshmen who traveled to Ireland. In her sorrow, Branwen had one consolation: a starling who visited her as she kneaded bread every day. She taught the starling to speak, then sent it to Brân with a message.

When Brân learned of his sister's disgrace and his countrymen's imprisonment, he summoned the hosts of the Isle of the Mighty. Nearly all the warriors of Britain set sail for Ireland. But Brân himself was a giant, too large to board any ship; he waded across the sea, carrying a troop of harpers on his back. Once in Ireland, the army came to an unnavigable and impassable river, but Brân said, "The chief shall be a bridge," and lay down across the river so that the hosts could cross on his back.

Seeing all this, Matholwch sought to appease Brân by abdicating his throne to Gwern. But at the feast to celebrate this treaty, Efnisien seized Gwern and threw him into the fire; Brân barely prevented Branwen from rushing into the flames after him. Fighting broke out immediately between the Irish and British. But the Irish had the advantage because they could throw their dead into the Cauldron of Rebirth; the warriors would spring out of it fully armed and ready to fight again. When Efnisien saw this, he lay among the Irish dead until he was thrown into the cauldron with them. Then he stretched himself and pushed against the cauldron sides until it burst.

At the end of the war, there were only five pregnant women left alive in Ireland. (The five sons they bore later became the founders of Ireland's "five fifths," or provinces.) The British host had only seven survivors, among them Pryderi, Taliesin, and Brân's brother Manawydan. Brân himself had been wounded by a poisoned spear. Because he could not live, he told the others to cut off his head and take it back to Britain with them and bury it on the White Hill in London. But first, he promised them, they would have many years of feasting.

The seven, with Branwen, returned to the Isle of the Mighty, landing first on Môn (Anglesey Island). Here Branwen died of a broken heart. The men buried her beside the Alaw River, and proceeded to Brân's hall in Harlech. For seven years they feasted there, and the birds of Rhiannon sang to them. Then the men went to the island of Gwales, off the south coast of Cornwall, where they feasted for 80 years with no memory of the sorrows they had suffered. All during this time, the head of Brân spoke to them, counseling and entertaining them. The head's companionship was as good as Brân's had been when he was alive, and so this gathering was known as the Assembly of the Noble Head.

At last the time came to return to their lives. They took the head to London and buried it, facing France, on the White Hill. That, according to Triad 37, was one of the Three Fortunate Concealments, for as long as the head remained where it was, no foreign oppression would ever come to the Island of Britain. Alas, King Arthur dug it up out of pride, for he wanted to hold the land by his own strength alone—and that was one of the Three Unfortunate Disclosures.

You can go to the White Hill today, where Brân's head once protected Britain from invasion; today it is called Tower Hill, and is the site of the Tower of London. If you visit, eventually a guide will point out to you the ravens of the Tower. There are always at least six of them, and it's said that if they ever leave, the Tower will fall and disaster will strike England. This legend has been around since at least the 1600s, and there's enough belief in it that every Tower raven has one wing clipped to prevent its flying away. Is it a coincidence that one of the Welsh words for "raven" is *brân*? We think not!

Clearly, one of Brân's most important aspects is as a protector of the land and its people. As a protector, he knows that his leadership includes an element of service: "The chief shall be a bridge"—one who upholds the people and ensures their well-being. In the context of Pagan Celtic religion, this proverb probably also meant that the chief was the living link between his people and the sacred land, and between his kingdom and the Otherworld. A good king was one under whom land and people prospered; if they did not, the king could lawfully be replaced. In the Second Branch, Brân's death makes way for a new king, but Brân remains Britain's ultimate protector, through the power of his severed head.

The Powers of the Wondrous Head

As we see in the Assembly of the Noble Head, protection is but one of the powers retained by Brân's head. This ties him in with one of the most notable aspects of ancient Celtic religion. The "cult of the head," as scholars typically call it, was known throughout the Celtic world. It was remarked on by classical writers, who described the Celts as "headhunters." For instance, the Roman historian Livy described Celts taking the head of a defeated Roman general and turning the skull into a gilded ritual cup; the Greek geographer Strabo told of Celtic warriors who proudly showed off the heads of especially worthy enemies, which they preserved in cedar oil and kept as family heirlooms in a special chest. Hundreds of years later, the Irish sagas tell of Cú Chulainn and other warriors taking heads as battle trophies and hanging them from their chariots or bridles.

Archaeological evidence for the cult of the head is abundant: In southern France, for example, a sanctuary gateway dating to the third century B.C.E. contains niches holding human skulls. Skulls have been found in many other settings, from the entries to forts to the bottoms of grain-storage pits. The human head is also one of the most common motifs in

Celtic sculpture and metalwork. Scholars generally agree that the use of the head in jewelry and horse fittings, and probably in other contexts, is meant to repel harm.

But why? What made the head such a potent symbol? Celticist Miranda Green (*The Gods of the Celts*, p. 32) says that we will never completely understand the importance of the head to the Celts, "but it was the means of identifying an individual, and was recognized as the power-centre for human action...it was clearly venerated as the most significant element in a human or divine image, representing the whole." We would add to this that, for the Celts, the head was not only regarded as the seat of thought, but also of emotion and will. A person's consciousness of her or his own individuality resided in the head, as did the personality and the spirit. The head was the sum and emblem of one's existence as an unique individual.

It may be that the severed head also symbolizes the divorcing of the spirit from the body at death. While the body decays, that which resides in the head is eternal. This would tie in with Brân's aspect as a god of the Otherworld. His affiliation with that realm is clear in one version of "The Battle of the Trees," in which he appears as the champion of Annwn. Moreover, the feast at which Brân's head presides is a type of Otherworld feast where there is neither memory of sorrow nor realization of time passing—just constant and enjoyable eating, drinking, conversation, poetry, and music.

In life, the head was seen as the governor of the body, similar to the way we understand the brain today. By metaphorical extension, the word for "head" was used to mean "chief, lord, prince, leader." In Welsh, *pen* means "head," and so, for example, we have Pwyll's title Pen Dyfed, "Prince of Dyfed." Another Welsh term probably connects with all of these ideas about the head: *wyneb,* "face," also means "honor." Like the Japanese, the Welsh had the concept of "losing face" if one's honor was insulted. *Wynebwerth* is an archaic Welsh word meaning "face price"—the compensation that someone must pay for insulting another.

It makes sense for the Noble Head to be connected with honor, and this is one of the themes that run through the Second Branch. The insult done to Matholwch through his horses sets off a tragic chain of events. As a guest in the land, he should be especially immune to such offenses, hospitality being one of the prime values of Celtic society. When a guest is dishonored, the host will be, too, unless he makes a suitable restitution. What Brân offers is a more than adequate recompense, and Matholwch accepts it gladly. Everything is restored to balance—until Matholwch's pride and greed get the better of him, and he leaves honor behind in his mistreatment of Branwen.

How many times do we, like Matholwch, take offense with someone for something that is not really his or her fault? How many times do we, like him, accept an apology, yet still not let the matter go? Almost nothing erodes honor and eats at the soul like holding a grudge. Even if we learn nothing else from the Second Branch (and there is so much in it!), we will be better for learning this.

Greed, grudges, and the like are barriers both to our well-being in the world and to our spiritual development. Fortunately, Brân is a breaker of barriers, a remover of obstacles. As a friend of ours puts it, "Nothing's going to get in the way of a guy who can wade the Irish Sea with a bunch of musicians on his back!" Brân offers us a path toward realizing our truest self, through noble service and the cultivation of the capabilities symbolized by the Wondrous Head.

Chapter 21

Taliesin:
The Divine Poet

We have encountered Taliesin already in this book, in the story of Ceridwen and Gwion Bach (Chapter 11). We left off that tale at the point when Ceridwen set her baby, the reborn Gwion, adrift in a little boat or hide-covered basket. Here is what happened next:

In some versions of the story, the baby floated on the waters for 40 years; in others, for only a few days. Either way, he ended up in the Conwy River near the sea, caught in a salmon weir. This particular weir was famous for trapping 10 (or 100) pounds of salmon without fail at the turning point of the year—either Nos Calan Gaeaf (Halloween/Samhain) or Nos Calan Mai (May Eve/Beltaine), depending on the particular rendition of the tale.

On the specified day, a penniless young noble named Elphin came to claim the contents of the weir, which had been granted him by his father, the weir's owner. Opening the fish trap, Elphin was amazed to find no salmon at all, but only something that looked like a leather bag. He cut it open, and the first thing he saw was the baby's forehead. It was so bright that Elphin exclaimed, "What a radiant (*iesin*) brow (*tal*)!" From that exclamation came the child's name: Taliesin.

As bright and beautiful as the baby was, however, Elphin was unhappy—he had needed the salmon to sell to pay his debts. Taliesin saw his sorrow and began to sing the poem known as "Elphin's Consolation," assuring him that he, Taliesin, was a far better catch than any fish and that, through his poetry, he would bring Elphin comfort, wealth, and honor.

And this is exactly what happened: Elphin's wealth increased with every passing day, and he became a favored courtier of the king. Meanwhile, he and his wife raised Taliesin as their own beloved son.

All went well for some years, until Elphin boasted at court that he had a wife of surpassing faithfulness and a bard (poet-singer) of greater skill than any of the king's bards. The king took offense, imprisoned Elphin, and sent his son to test Elphin's wife's faithfulness. Luckily, Taliesin had the gift of foreknowledge, warned his foster mother, and foiled the plans of the would-be seducer. Then he set off for court to prove the second part of Elphin's boast.

The king was holding a great feast, and Taliesin settled himself off to the side. As each of the bards and minstrels passed him on their way to appear before the king, Taliesin strummed his pursed lips with his fingers. Because of his magic, the bards were unable to sing or recite for the king, but could only do as Taliesin had done, making a sound like *blerum blerum*. When the king accused them of being drunk, his chief bard promptly put the blame on Taliesin.

The king summoned and questioned Taliesin, who answered him with a series of poems. He sang a poem that raised a great wind, which shook the castle. This persuaded the king to release Elphin from prison, and then Taliesin sang another poem that unlocked the chains that bound Elphin. His next poems challenged and satirized the king's pompous bards, effectively silencing them. They were "bards of limited horizons"—but he, Taliesin, was Chief Bard of the Western World.

The Omnipresent Poet

This is the only tale in which Taliesin is a central figure, but looking at other Welsh sources, we find him almost everywhere. He is one of the survivors of the war in Ireland in the Second Branch of the Mabinogi; in the poem "Cad Goddeu" he is a companion of Gwydion. He shows up repeatedly as a member of King Arthur's retinue: in the Triads, in the story "Culhwch and Olwen," and in the poem "The Spoils of Annwn."

As we have seen, the story of Taliesin depicts him as poet, seer, and magician, with a bit of trickster thrown in. He is in some ways similar to Gwydion, to whom he sometimes compares himself. In fact, he makes all kinds of assertions in his poems, placing himself in all times, places, and things.

Here is a typical example, from Patrick K. Ford's 1977 translation of "Cad Goddeu" ("The Battle of the Trees"):

> I was lanterns of light for a year and a half;
> I was a bridge that stretched over sixty estuaries;
> I was a path, I was an eagle, I was a coracle in seas;
> I was a bubble in beer, I was a drop in a shower;
> I was a sword in hand, I was a shield in battle;
> I was a string in a harp enchanted nine years, in the water as foam;
> I was a spark in fire, I was wood in a bonfire;
> I am not one who does not sing; I have sung since I was small.

In many of the Taliesin poems, the poet also speaks of having been present at events in biblical and classical history, such as Noah's flood and the fall of Troy. Some people find these non-Celtic references a source of frustration. But a possible interpretation of their presence in the tradition is that Taliesin was such an awe-inspiring figure, occupying such a major place in British lore, that the medieval Welsh felt he must have been present in *every* circumstance that affected their nation. In other words, it was simply part of Taliesin's nature to be all-encompassing.

To understand why Taliesin looms so large in Welsh tradition, we need to know something of how the Celts thought about poetry and poets. Among Celtic-speaking peoples during the ancient and early-medieval periods (and, to a lesser extent, even later), poetry was closely linked with prophecy and magic. Irish tradition makes this explicit: The word for the best-educated type of poet was *fili* (plu., *filid*), which also meant "seer." A poet's training opened him (occasionally, her) to receive inspiration, which brought with it wisdom and knowledge that were unavailable to ordinary people. Poets of high rank were expected not only to entertain and praise the nobles or communities they served, but also to advise them.

Celtic poetry (like that of many cultures) employed a heightened and intensified form of language, using structures and often even words very different from those of everyday speech. This special poetic language was the one most suitable for communicating insights from the Otherworld (prophecy) or effecting change among the people of this world (magic). Celtic poets went through long years of training and perhaps initiation rituals like those hinted at in the story of Ceridwen and Gwion Bach to learn to use this language appropriately, effectively, and spontaneously.

The early Celtic poet's art was an oral one. Poems were spoken or sung aloud in a public setting. A Greco-Roman author of the second century C.E. wrote that when he was in Gaul, a Celt explained to him that eloquence was as mighty as Hercules. Words had power, and a poet's utterance could both create and destroy. If a poet said that a ruler was brave and generous, that became the truth—because the ruler had to keep his (or, occasionally, her) reputation for these qualities in order to continue to lead the people. If a poet satirized a ruler, declared him a coward or miser, the people would lose confidence, would stop following him, and might demand a new leader. Satire, it was believed, could even permanently disfigure its victim. No wonder that one of the Welsh words for "poet," *prydydd*, literally means "shaper"—a trained and inspired poet was truly capable of reshaping the world around him by means of the words he uttered.

The power of the words was amplified by the element of music. Classical authors noted that the Celtic poets and singers called bards played "an instrument like the lyre" to accompany their songs. For bards of later times, we know, the harp was their signature instrument. And by the early Middle Ages, the title for the highest-ranking bard at a British king's court was *pencerdd*, "chief of song." Melody, rhythm, rhyme, repetition, and all the other elements of traditional poetry and song combined to make the words of the bards both powerful and memorable.

To be worthy of memory was a prime goal of Celtic nobles and rulers. And it was the bards and *filid* who had the greatest power to keep someone alive in the memory of the people. The ancient Celts did not write down their myths, legends, histories, or philosophy. Such lore was regarded as sacred knowledge, and so had to be preserved in the head. Poets in training were required to memorize genealogies, history, stories, geography, traditions about local landmarks, and so on. It was their responsibility to preserve all the knowledge of their people. A bard was the embodiment of memory, and this is another reason why the mystical Taliesin poems portray him as a witness or participant in every step of the path from past to present.

Inspiration and Transformation

Taliesin is a complicated character indeed. For one thing, we know that a poet named Taliesin lived in the kingdom of Rheged (today, southern Scotland and northern England) toward the end of the sixth century. He was a celebrated bard attached to the royal court, and several of his praise poems to kings and great lords survive. The relationship between this figure and the Taliesin of legend has been a subject of great debate— and probably we will never know the exact truth. There was a long-standing Welsh tradition, however, that Taliesin was one of several incarnations of Merlin—who himself was "a spirit in human form." And as late as the 16th century, this spirit was "said to be resting in Caer Sidia [sic], whence certain people believe firmly that he will rise up once again before doomsday" (Ford, *Ystoria Taliesin*, p. 4).

Indeed, in one of the mythically oriented Taliesin poems, the poet says, "My chair is in Caer Sidi"—one of the regions of Annwn, the Otherworld; Annwn, where nine maidens guard a pearl-rimmed cauldron, warming it with their breath. Once more we are reminded of the Cauldron of Ceridwen and its brew filled with wisdom and the spirit of prophecy. This was the *awen* ("inspiration"), and when Gwion Bach swallowed it, it became part of him. By its power, he was transformed, becoming Taliesin, the Primary Bard (*prifardd*), who embodied the *awen*: wisdom and the spirit of prophecy, in human form and in all the ages.

Awen has the power, at least for a time, to turn ordinary humans into something more, something able to partake of and communicate Otherworld knowledge. In the 12th century, Giraldus Cambrensis described people known as Awenyddion, diviners who went into a frenzy and gave forth mysterious but wonderful-sounding utterances, as though some under-world spirit had entered them and spoke through them; this gift came to them through visions they had at night while sleeping. Still later historical records tell us that part of the training for poets in Scotland and Ireland involved being shut in a completely dark room all day, lying with a heavy stone on the belly to prevent movement while composing verses. At root, this must be a kind of symbolic death; a ritual of passage into the Otherworld. At the same time, it could symbolize a return to the womb. "I was nine months gestating / in the witch Ceridwen. / Gwion Bach I was then, / but now I'm Taliesin!" (Ford, *The Celtic Poets*, p. 25).

Taliesin shows that a truly inspired poet is one who gives up the ordinary life of "small horizons." Instead, the poet must cultivate and embrace the *awen*, with a willingness to explore the depths of being and to come back from this quest transformed, and all in the service of the divine. The *awen* transforms consciousness, imparting a heightened awareness that perceives the connections among different planes, realms, or states of being. Eventually, the *awen* builds up inside to the point where it must express itself in words, and the poet has gone from being a Gwion Bach to a Taliesin. The poetry itself may then become the *awen*—and those who encounter these words stand themselves in the place of Gwion, waiting to receive their own three drops from the Cauldron of Wisdom.

Taliesin and Sacred Time

As we have seen, the existing versions of Taliesin's story place his birth/ rebirth either on October 31 (Nos Calan Gaeaf/Samhain) or April 30 (Nos Calan Mai/Beltaine Eve). These, remember, are the times when the veil between the Otherworld and this one is at its thinnest. Gestating in the womb of Ceridwen, Taliesin is in the Otherworld. Then, in his little hide-covered boat, he floats upon the current that runs between worlds. The salmon weir, where he comes to rest on a magical day, is a point of contact between the two worlds. Expecting to find one kind of gift in the weir, Elphin (a fairly average sort of person) finds something completely different, but, he will discover, more precious than anything he could have imagined. The gifts of the Otherworld are rarely just what we expect. Even as a baby, Taliesin is the embodiment of the Otherworld gifts of poetry, wisdom, and prophecy. Radiant, he is an enlightener of humanity.

Taliesin's radiant nature can also be seen to connect him with the sun. In this aspect, we might favor April 30 as his birth date. In the Celtic calendar, this marks the beginning of summer, the season of the sun's greatest strength. Some Wiccan groups also like February 1 (Imbolc) as a time to honor Taliesin, in part because this is about the time when it becomes very obvious that the days are longer than the nights: the sun is overcoming the darkness. This is, moreover, one of the days that country people in Wales traditionally celebrated with poetry contests, where poetry was improvised on the spot. What an excellent way to honor Taliesin!

Every Day with Taliesin

Poetry, alas, has become a marginal art form in our society. But if we want to show devotion to Taliesin, we need first and foremost to give poetry a more central place in our lives. And this means more than simply expressing our emotions in free verse in our journals—although that can be a start. Celtic bards were steeped in tradition, and so we should follow their example and read as much of the poetry written by them and their descendants as we can.

Of course, it can be difficult to track down works by medieval poets (whether in the original language or in translation), but many modern poets from Celtic countries have written in English and so are easily accessible. Among them are William Butler Yeats, Dylan Thomas, Seamus Heaney, Paul Muldoon, Eavan Boland, and Robin Williamson (who has also issued CDs in which he recites ancient Celtic stories and poems to the accompaniment of his harp). Read their works aloud or, when possible, listen to recordings they have made of their readings. Sound—vibration carried by the air—is an important component of Celtic (and much other) poetry, and we often miss out on it by silently reading the words on a page.

To write poetry in the spirit of Taliesin, you must get into the habit of thinking like a bard. Look for the connections between things: the connections between nature and humanity; between the Otherworld and this world; between the past, present, and future; between individuals. Contemplate the essences of things and what you share with them. Where does the divine make itself manifest? The insights you will gain as you pursue this path are among the treasures of the Otherworld, and they have the power to transform you. Then, if you truly open yourself to the *awen*, you will find the words that allow you to bring those treasures back to this world.

Part Four:

Goddesses and Gods in Our Lives

Chapter 22

The Mysteries
and the Virtues

Learning about some of the Celtic deities is only the first step toward
a rich and full spirituality centered on the old ways. Remember,
the gods and goddesses presented in this book represent a fraction of the
Celtic community of deities—and we have by no means been exhaustive in
sharing the stories or qualities associated with the gods and goddesses we
covered. So it is important for anyone interested in these deities to make
studying and learning the myths and lore a continual priority (see the
appendices for some ideas of where to go after you finish this book).

In this chapter and the two that follow, we would like to give some
additional ideas for cultivating a deeper Celtic spirituality. Bearing in mind
the promise that we made in Chapter 3—it is not our intention to dictate
beliefs—we hope you will consider the ideas presented here and see if you
can incorporate them meaningfully into your own practice of honoring the
deities.

Magic and Mysticism

Much of the Neo-Pagan community has tended to approach the gods
and goddesses from a primarily magical perspective. This involves relating
to the deities in terms of spiritual power; in other words, focusing on the
energies that the gods and goddesses provide for the manifestation and
achievement of spiritual or mundane goals. Part of the beauty of Paganism
is how positive and affirming it is in this regard—where other religions can

sometimes be heavy-handed in their message of self-denial, Paganism condones and even celebrates the use of spiritual energy for taking care of oneself, just because it's a good thing to do so.

On our journey exploring the world of the Celtic deities, however, we'd like to offer something beyond the traditional Pagan understanding of magic. That "something beyond" is *mysticism*, a practice that is centered not on personal fulfillment, but on devotion to the gods and goddesses for *their* sake. Think of it this way: Magic emphasizes what the gods and goddesses can do for you; mysticism emphasizes what you do for them. These two aspects of Paganism need not be contradictory or mutually exclusive. Indeed, the strongest and most balanced spirituality generally incorporates both magical and mystical qualities.

Before going any further, here's an important point about language: Many traditional teachers of magical religion do offer their students guidance in mystical spirituality (sometimes referring to its practice as high magic). Both *magic* and *mysticism* are words used in a broad number of ways, often describing widely different or even contradictory aspects of spirituality. We don't really want to go down the rabbit hole of trying to find the most perfect or precise definitions of these conceptually complex words. Let's just say that, *for the purposes of this book*, we're defining *magic* as "the spirituality of personal fulfillment" and *mysticism* as "the spirituality of profound relationship with the gods." If, in your mind, mysticism is actually a subset of magic, that's fine with us. After all, forming a true relationship with the gods *is* a personally fulfilling experience. Therefore, mysticism can truly be understood as an aspect of magic. In fact, some teachers would insist that such spiritual qualities as mysticism, devotion, and meditation are the *most important* parts of magic!

Defining Mysticism

Just what is *mysticism*? The word comes from the Greek *mystes*, which literally means "one who has been initiated." Initiation, in this sense, involves entry into the *mysteries*—a religious term that originally meant "spiritual truths beyond human understanding." Remember in Chapter 3 when we looked at many possible ways to think about or believe in the gods and goddesses? We could approach them as psychological archetypes, as aspects of the "One Spirit;" as ancestral beings who were enlightened and/or avatars, and so on. You might have come away from that chapter wondering,

"But what is the *truth*?" To which we would reply, "Ultimately, no one knows." The true nature of the gods and goddesses is a mystery. The "truth" of the deities lies beyond human understanding, and our various beliefs are nothing more than theories about the mystery.

Spiritual mysteries take us beyond the limits of human thought and imagination and experience, where our mortal and temporal consciousness is free to encounter—and merge into—the undying and eternal presence of the divine. Entering into the mysteries means more than just learning about the gods, or performing rituals dedicated to them, or even experiencing a sense of their presence in our lives. It means opening ourselves up to the deities, offering ourselves in such a way that we become available for an intimate and transformational relationship with them, *on their terms*; in other words, a relationship that transcends even the limits of our thoughts and feelings.

One of the most common fallacies about mysticism is that it's concerned with spiritual experience. Because mysticism takes us beyond the limits of human understanding and experience, the power of mysticism is not something we can fully feel or comprehend. This doesn't mean we give up on the idea of seeking to experience the gods in our lives. Remember, pursuing mysticism doesn't mean that we abandon magic. We can still benefit from rituals and spells and guided meditations that promise to help us cultivate a sense of divine energy flowing through us, experienced in physical, mental, and emotional ways. But the pursuit of mystical spirituality means that the full impact of whom the gods are and how they make a difference for us goes *far beyond* just the drama of our own experience. It means inviting the gods to transform our lives in ways that we may not even be aware of—to guide the highest dimensions of our superconscious mind (sometimes called the higher self), and to cultivate their divine values and virtues within us, literally remaking us as custodians of divine energy in the world.

Think of mystical spirituality this way: Through devotion to the gods, through meditation, through surrendering to the power of the gods and goddesses that flows through us in ways beyond what our conscious minds can comprehend, we are offering ourselves to become members of the divine family—to join our ancestors and the spirits of nature and the gods themselves as conduits through which the energies of the gods and goddesses flow into all areas of our lives. This means that in all our choices, commitments, relationships, and creativity—from momentous decisions down to the most seemingly immaterial choices we make—we become agents of the gods and goddesses in manifesting their power and joy and love and healing presence in the world.

Elements of Mystical Spirituality

Well, how do we go about pursuing a mystical relationship with the deities? There are several important elements to mysticism of any kind, including Pagan mysticism:

- ∞ *Meditation*: Disciplining the mind to enter heightened or altered states of consciousness, thereby facilitating greater receptivity to the gods. (This, incidentally, is not only the key to mysticism, but the key to magic as well. In magic, meditation is a way of focusing the mind's energy; in mysticism, it is a way of opening up the mind to receive the energies that the gods seek to give us.)

- ∞ *Devotion*: Orienting our thoughts and feelings toward loving and caring for the deities, putting their needs and concerns and perspectives ahead of our own, even if only for a set period of time (see Chapter 23 for more on this important topic).

- ∞ *Prayer*: Using conscious thought to create intimacy and relatedness with the gods by disclosing our ideas and feelings and asking for the gods' attention.

- ∞ *Ritual*: Here's where magic (as it is commonly understood) and mysticism come together. Through ceremonial practices, we can formally nurture a sense of relationship to the gods. Just as a husband and wife use rituals to express their love for one another (a glass of wine together every night before going to bed; roses on Valentine's Day), we can also strengthen our mystical connection with the gods through regular rituals in our lives. Rituals can include praise, thanksgiving, prayer, meditation, chants, spells, and devotion to the deities—in other words, all the key elements of magic and mysticism, integrated in a single act of conscious (and beyond-conscious) connection to the deities.

- ∞ *Study*: Taking the time to get to know the gods and goddesses; not just what their magical correspondences are, but truly knowing their stories, as recounted in myth and legend throughout history. This also includes getting to know what contemporary devotees to the gods and goddesses are thinking and saying about them.

❧ *Virtue*: Most gods and goddesses expect their devotees to behave in certain ways. *Virtues* is a word that many people confuse with *morals*—but virtues are not necessarily rules for restrained conduct. Rather, they are values that can help us to live effectively and powerfully. Virtues define who we are, what we believe, and how we conduct our lives.

The Path of Virtue

Virtue is such an important (and again, often underemphasized) element of Pagan mysticism that it deserves some further attention. The pursuit of virtue does not mean that we all must become Pagan do-gooders. It *does* mean that we have a responsibility to live according to our highest principles (or, in spiritual terms, to order our lives according to the values expressed by our gods). It means being conscious of what our deepest and most authentic desires are and structuring our lives so that we can be faithful to what matters the most to us. For many Pagans, this could include having a connection to the gods and the ancestors and the spirits of nature; finding happiness; living in a balanced relationship with the earth; being faithful to those we love and nurturing our family or community or tribe so that everyone prospers; and leaving the world a better place than we found it, as a gift to our children and grandchildren. Once again, it's not our intention to tell you what to believe—so take the time to get to know *your* deepest principles and values.

Part of the beauty and power of developing a mystical relationship with the gods is that they are willing (some would say eager) to bestow their blessings on those who are devoted to them. Chief among the blessings we can receive from the gods are the virtues and values necessary to live in harmony with them. Think of mysticism as a loving relationship, in which you give the gods your devotion, meditative energy, and sense of commitment, and they in turn give you energy for empowered living and a sense of the values and virtues necessary to live your life well.

To truly enter into the mysteries of the gods, we need to know the virtues that each one looks for in his or her devotees. And yes, the virtues vary from deity to deity. For example, the Morrígan expects her devotees to be committed to their principles and willing to fight for what they believe in, while Brigit particularly bestows her favor on those who work for peace and conflict resolution. This doesn't mean you can't be devoted to both goddesses. But if you are, you need to be very clear about the balance between the warrior and the peacemaker within your own life.

Here is a list of some virtues that are specific to deities discussed in this book. Notice there is some overlap, but plenty of variety, too. One way for you, as a seeker of Celtic spirituality, to decide which gods or goddesses you wish to cultivate a stronger relationship with is to consider which virtues or values are important to you—or, which virtues and values you want more of in your life.

Particular virtues related to specific deities include:

Anu: Love for the land, environmental responsibility

Arianrhod: Ability to set limits, turning obstacles into opportunities

Boann: Thirst for wisdom, willingness to break the rules

Brân: Responsibility, caring for others, "bridge building"

Brigit: Compassion, healing, peacemaking

Ceridwen: Wisdom, motherly love, inspiration

Cernunnos: Wildness, care for the environment, daring

Cú Chulainn: Honor, discipline, self-sacrifice

The Dagda: Generosity, humility, earthiness

Gwydion: Intelligence, perceptivity, ability to learn from mistakes

Lleu: Sacrifice, skill, trust

Lugh: Justice, leadership, valor

Macha: Honor, athletic skill

Manannán: Devotion, forgiveness, faithfulness

Manawydan: Discretion, balance, responsibility

Medb: Eroticism, generosity, non-jealousy

The Morrigán: Courage, valor, eroticism

The Mothers: Generosity, nurturing

Oenghus: Romantic love, perseverance, self-sacrifice

Rhiannon: Care for animals, endurance, graciousness

Taliesin: Eloquence, transformation, creativity

As you explore your relationship with the gods and goddesses, both through study and through spiritual work such as ritual and meditation, you will discover other virtues associated with the various ones you revere.

The more connected you become to these deities, the more powerfully the energies of their virtues will flow through your life.

What the Gods Expect From You

You may have noticed that we began our discussion of virtues by talking about the gods expecting certain behaviors from us. If you want to have a close and spiritually satisfying relationship with the deities, it won't be a one-way street. You can expect blessings and magic from the gods—but what will *they* expect from you in return? Pagan spirituality is based on traditional values. Celtic mythology abounds in tales that express the importance of virtues such as hospitality, honor, courage, and wisdom. Again and again, the goddesses reveal the importance of *sovereignty* (freedom) in the Pagan life, while the heroic gods remind us of the necessity to defend Lady Sovereignty from those who would attack her.

Neo-Pagans in the 21st century, unlike our ancient forebears, do not always do a very good job at considering what our duties are as Pagans. After all, we live in a culture that places much more of an emphasis on rights than on responsibilities. In our rush to safeguard what we believe we deserve, all too often it seems we have mindlessly ignored the higher calling—what is expected of us, as citizens of the planet and kinsmen and kinswomen of the natural world, the ancestors and the deities.

There's no time like the present to address this imbalance and to consider how we, as Neo-Pagans, can give back to those who have created, sustained, and empowered or enriched our lives. To get us started, here are a few ideas of what the Celtic gods and goddesses, speaking in general terms, might request from their devotees. Don't just take our word for it, though—explore this topic further through your rituals and meditations. Ask the gods to guide you.

> ❧ *The gods and goddesses expect you to take care of nature (including your own nature).* If the goddess represents the sovereignty of the land—and our freedom in relation to it—then it's logical to assume the goddess is very interested in the well-being of the land she embodies. Meanwhile, a heroic god who stands tall and proud in his role as guardian of the land would have a similar viewpoint. As Neo-Pagans, we share in their divine relationship with the land—and by extension, with all of nature. If something exists in nature, it deserves to

be treated with honor and respect. This includes not only the wilderness, the ocean, and the atmosphere, but also those aspects of "nature" that are closer to home, such as our homes, our neighborhoods, and our bodies. In other words, Neo-Paganism is not only about recycling and using "green" products, it's also about eating healthy, organic food, refraining from addictions, and getting proper amounts of rest and exercise.

🙰 *The gods and goddesses expect you to make wise and virtuous choices.* Contrary to what some people may think, Paganism is not an "anything goes" spiritual path. Our ancestors had very clear ideas about right and wrong, and were vigilant in protecting the safety and holiness of their community through correct behavior. We may live in an age of situation ethics and moral relativism, but all that means is that we take responsibility for thinking through the complex issues in our lives. Being a Pagan doesn't excuse us from commonsense rules of conduct. Lying, stealing, and cheating are just as immoral for Pagans as for anyone else. The same can be said for addictions to alcohol, nicotine, gambling, or pornography. Even something that is good or morally neutral becomes a problem when it is abused, or used in a way that hurts yourself or other people. The Pagan path is built on the solid values that have guided all civilizations: honesty, fairness, personal responsibility, and respect for others and others' property. On a related note, just because you become devoted to Celtic spirituality or to one particular deity does not excuse you from all the other important values that hold society together. If the Dagda is your patron, you don't have a license to abuse your body with overeating! Moreover, following the Celtic path does not exempt us from such basics as kindness, fairness, and forgiveness.

🙰 *The gods and goddesses expect you to live up to your commitments (including your commitments to them).* For example, as a devotee to Brigit, you would want to live in ways that foster creativity and healing (both for yourself and others). Or as a devotee to the Morrigán, you would make the effort to achieve peak physical fitness, a strong and confident ability to defend yourself and others if necessary, and a keen sense of the code of the warrior (using your strength in the service of good, not merely as a tool for self-service). We cannot emphasize this enough: You honor the gods and goddesses not only by how you think, but also by how you live your life.

This list, clearly, is only a start. We'll leave it up to you to explore the deities' expectations further. If you disagree with our ideas of what the gods expect, that's your prerogative. But know *why* you disagree. Are you put off by the idea that spirituality includes a measure of obligation and commitment? Or perhaps you feel that there is an important philosophical, ethical, or theological reason to disagree with our ideas. As part of your journey toward deeper connection with the old gods and goddesses, we encourage you to consider carefully the implications and consequences of your attitudes and beliefs.

A Final Word

Earlier in this chapter, we insisted that mystical spirituality is about more than just what we experience in meditation or ritual. As we learn to exercise virtues and values and strive to live according to the expectations of our deities, we are continually offering them energy that they can use to bless us, in ways we can never fully understand. But if mysticism involves a spiritual dimension beyond what we can even experience, then why bother? We can only offer a short answer here: because it makes a difference. Mystical spirituality makes magic more effective, ritual more powerful, life more vibrant with the unseen but intuitively known presence of the gods. This is not something that can be put into words. But if you seek to walk the mystical path, you *will* receive blessings.

 Chapter 23

Putting Devotion into Practice

By sharing some of the results of our own research, insights, and experiences with Celtic goddesses and gods, we hope this book will inspire you to work further with them. To learn and explore more, we recommend that next you read or reread the deities' full mythologies. For those goddesses and gods with no existing written myths (such as the Mothers and Cernunnos), you will find sculptures and other artwork depicting them reproduced in many Celtic studies books. But don't just seek the deities in books—look for them in nature and in your own life.

Cultivating Mindfulness

Mindfulness is an important part of spiritual practice in many religions. In the Celtic traditions, the worlds of spirit and matter are constantly interacting. This dynamic is at its strongest and most volatile at Samhain and Beltaine, but there is never a time that does not hold the potential for us to the touch the divine—and vice versa. All it takes is attuning our minds (and our hearts and our wills) to the possibility.

Throughout this book, we've talked about various deities' fields of interest or areas of patronage. This information may help you to choose a goddess or god to pray to in a particular situation. Or, if you practice a magical tradition, you may wish to invoke deities who are appropriate to the goals of your magic. (Religious magic, by the way, is in our view simply an active form of focused prayer.) Remember, though, that the gods and goddesses are not at our beck and call and that we owe them respect and honor. Also, remember that while spiritual action can effect great changes, physical action is usually necessary, too—no amount of prayer or spellwork is going to get you a job, for example, if you're not also answering want ads, sending out your resume, cultivating your professional contacts, etc.

Our hope is that you can use the information we've given about various deities not just so you know whom to turn to when you're in need of divine assistance, but also so you can deepen the spiritual dimension of your life. For instance, the simple act of putting a bandage on a child's skinned knee can be an act of devotion to Brigit in her aspect as a goddess of healing. If you are thinking of Brigit—even for only a couple of seconds—as you stick on that Band-Aid, then you are bringing more of her divine energy into manifestation in your life. And you are forging a stronger connection between your everyday existence and the divine.

Folk prayers from Scotland and Ireland have long been a means of bringing divine energy into the common events of life. These prayers have been preserved mainly in Christianized forms, especially in the folklore collection known as *Carmina Gadelica*. The pre-Christian root of such devotions is often apparent, making them valuable spiritual tools for Neo-Pagans. For example, a prayer said while banking the hearth fire for the night goes:

> I will smoor the hearth
> As Brigit the Foster-mother would smoor.
> The foster-mother's holy name
> Be on the hearth, be on the herd,
> Be on the household all.

This prayer formula is open to many adaptations. For example, if you are leaving on a business trip (and particularly if you are a nervous traveler), you might pray, "As Manawydan traveled far from his land to pursue his work, so I am traveling. As Manawydan returned to his land and was reunited with his family, so I will return, successful in my work, and my family and I together in our home."

This technique is probably even more beneficial the more commonplace the circumstances. It's too easy to forget that the divine has anything to do with our mundane lives, but such simple prayers can help "re-enchant" the ordinary rhythms of the day. Try saying to yourself when you get up for work on Monday morning, "As Manawydan began another day of sewing shoes, so I am beginning my workday; as he labored honestly and to the best of his ability, so will I." Or, when you are cooking supper: "Just as Ceridwen prepared her cauldron to benefit her son, so I am stirring this pot of food so that my children will thrive." If you read the myths carefully, you will get many other ideas for "divine parallels" that fit your life and circumstances. Experiencing the harmony between your life and the "lives" of the deities makes for an ever-deepening sense of connection between yourself and the divine. This is prayerful or mindful living—or, as Joseph Campbell might have said, "living mythically."

We can also cultivate mindfulness by appealing to our five senses. Many deities have certain plants, animals, symbols, or colors associated with them. For example, we have mentioned that roses were used in the worship of Epona—so a rose perfume or incense could help you be more mindful of the energy of Epona/Rhiannon. A silver necklace could be used to keep you mindful of Arianrhod, not only when you glimpse yourself in the mirror, but also when you are conscious of the feel of the necklace against your skin. The light and heat of a candle flame can connect you to Brigit. Listening to a performance or recording of Celtic harp music, of course, would easily put you in mind of Taliesin.

An altar is an excellent tool for mindfulness. You can use a shelf, a tabletop, the top of your dresser, even a corner of your desk—any bit of clear, flat surface. If possible, you want to situate your altar in a spot where you will see it throughout the day or where you will have to at least walk past it frequently as you go about your daily routine. So, while an altar in an isolated nook in your garden will be very beautiful and spiritual, it is probably not a practical choice if you are using the altar to cultivate mindfulness (unless you spend a large amount of time in the garden every day).

Your altar can be as discreet as need be, with perhaps only a couple of symbolic objects, or as elaborate as your circumstances permit. There is no right or wrong way to set it up—this is all about *your* connection to the goddesses and gods. You might start with an altar cloth of a color that is associated with the deity for whom you are cultivating mindfulness. If you have a picture or statue of the deity, you can add that. The goddess or god might be linked to a particular animal—for example, the eagle for Lleu Llaw Gyffes, the raven for Brân—so a picture or model of that creature can go on your altar, too. Is there a particular place associated with the deity? Maybe you have a photo, postcard, or magazine picture of it. What about plants or flowers? You might place some in a vase. Or, a bowl of potpourri or a scented candle can bring your sense of smell into play. A large range of symbolic objects are possible—for instance, a seashell for Manannán, a mousetrap for Manawydan. (Extra points for creativity!)

If you don't have a place where you can physically set up an altar, use your imagination to set it up in your mind. Take your time selecting and picturing all its details. You can work at it over the course of many days or even weeks. Just call its image to mind whenever you have an idle moment and your brain is otherwise unoccupied. In fact, this is an excellent exercise to work on even if you have a physical altar. After all, you can take your mental altar with you wherever you go.

Devotionals

Setting up an altar is generally one of the steps in preparing for a devotional. This is a ritual or meditation that is designed to bring you into closer communion with a particular deity. The preparation is in fact part of the ritual, so it should not be rushed; take a week or even longer to gather the altar dressing and other things you will use in your devotional. This process keeps you mindful.

Devotionals are individualized and open-ended. You must take into account your own needs and abilities as well as the character of the goddess or god you are approaching. Start by deciding which deity you would like to connect with more deeply, then choose a time and place when you will do your devotional. Also, be alert to opportunities that may offer themselves for getting to know various deities better. For instance, if you have a camping trip coming up, you might plan to set aside time for a devotional to Cernunnos while you are in the woods.

Chances are you will do most of your devotionals indoors. Gather together everything you can think of that symbolizes the particular deity to you. Don't feel you have to go out and buy things; this is not about getting more stuff! It's more important to look at what's around you and see how it might relate to various goddesses and gods. Be alert for serendipity—while you are planning a devotional to Lleu Llaw Gyffes, for example, you might come across some fallen oak leaves or acorns, which would key into the part of the myth in which Lleu in eagle form is perched in an oak tree.

As you gather your deity symbols, add them to your altar or put them together in a safe place. Finally, if practical, you'll want to have a candle of an appropriate color (but white or natural beeswax will always work fine). You may also want to use incense—if possible, it is always best to make your own—and/or an appropriate essential oil.[1] The sense of smell works very powerfully on our emotions and memories, so involving it in a devotional can really strengthen the experience. You may also wish to bring in your sense of hearing; if you plan to play a tape or CD during your devotional, it's generally best to choose one that's all instrumental (words are likely to distract you) and keep the volume low.

The time for your devotional has come. If you haven't been able to set up an altar, improvise one by spreading out a cloth on the floor (or on your bed or whatever you have to work with), and arrange your symbolic objects on it. If you cast a circle when you do magical work, go ahead and do so. Otherwise, simply acknowledge to yourself that you are now stepping into a time and space that are set apart, where you are safe and watched over by the goddesses and gods.

Sit comfortably before your altar, with your spine as straight as possible and the rest of your body feeling "loose"—you want your body relaxed but energized. If you are using a candle and/or incense, go ahead and light them. Anoint yourself with your essential oil, if you have one. (If you don't have a standard way of anointing, just put a bit of oil on your fingertip and touch it to your forehead, heart, and belly.) Slow your breathing, and breathe deeply and evenly—for example, inhale to a slow count of four and exhale to a slow count of four; after a few cycles, the rhythm will become natural and you won't have to count anymore. Focus your thoughts on the deity you have chosen to work with, and allow yourself only to think about things to do with her or him. If other thoughts creep in, just let them pass through, or gently push them aside, and then return your focus to your deity.

What happens from here on is up to you and your goddess or god. You may wish to just silently contemplate the various symbols you've gathered. You could simply chant the deity's name, or you might sing a chant or recite a poem that has to do with this goddess or god. If you are musically inclined, you could drum or play an appropriate tune or improvise on the instrument of your choice. (This is especially good if you're seeking to connect with Taliesin.) You might tell part of the deity's story aloud to yourself. You could visualize the story as a kind of movie—in which you might even play a bit part (for instance, the rider who first pursues Rhiannon on Pwyll's behalf). If you are approaching a warrior deity and you have martial arts training, it might be appropriate to get up and do one of your forms. There are a variety of ways to connect with the goddesses and gods; your reading of the myths and your imagination will give you many more ideas.

Every devotional is going to be different. Most of the time, though, you will find yourself ending in silence, contemplating the deity. You may then experience a flash of vision, or attain an insight, or hear the deity telling you something, or simply feel a deep sense of connectedness. Some people even hold brief "conversations" with the goddesses and gods for whom they perform devotionals. And for some people, it seems like "nothing" happens. But if you have really sought to connect with a deity, *something* will happen. It may be a subtle change that occurs over time, until one day you wake up and realize (after a devotional to Medb, for instance), "Wow, I've become a lot more assertive in the last year!"

When you are done with your devotional (trust yourself to sense this), thank the deity for her or his attention—and for anything specific that may have occurred during the devotional. If you've cast a circle, proceed as you normally would at the end of ritual. Otherwise, gently (say, to a slow count of five) bring yourself back to your normal state of consciousness. Wiggle your fingers and toes; roll your shoulders; stretch. Do something, like snapping your fingers three times, that works as a signal to your mind and body that you have returned to the mundane here-and-now. If you still feel a little "out of it," have a bite to eat—especially something with protein—to ground yourself again in physical reality.

You can do as many devotionals as you like to a single deity, and you can do devotionals to as many deities as you like. You will learn from them all. Eventually, you may develop a special relationship with one or a few deities—those who seem to especially watch over your life, who have particular lessons to teach you. You may feel instinctively drawn to a patron goddess or god, or you may consciously seek to honor and emulate a deity in the way you live your life. And sometimes, for reasons that may not be obvious, you may feel that a particular deity has chosen you. Embrace this opportunity; you will learn and grow in spirit and become a better tool for manifesting divine energy in the world. And doesn't the world need more of that?

Chapter 24

Storytelling and
the Living Tradition

Throughout this book we've described various ways of deepening your connection with the goddesses and gods and of "walking your talk" with regard to them. In this final chapter, we want to focus on the power of story. We mentioned, toward the beginning of this journey, that storytelling allows you to encounter the deities in their own habitat, so to speak. Now we're going to explore that habitat a little further.

Our word *story* comes ultimately from Greek *historia*, "researches" or "inquiries"—this is the sense in which Herodotus, the first great Greek historian, used the term. *Historia* itself comes from the root *histor* or *istor*, meaning "knowing" or "learned." So at its most ancient heart, story is about learning, about seeking knowledge. The Welsh language also makes this connection, and more, according to Alwyn and Brinley Rees in their important book *Celtic Heritage* (p. 212): "The old Welsh word for 'story,' *cyfarwyddyd*, means 'guidance,' 'direction,' 'instruction,' 'knowledge,' 'skill,' 'prescription.' Its stem, *arwydd*, means 'sign,' 'symbol,' 'manifestation,' 'omen,' 'miracle,' and derives from a root meaning 'to see.' The storyteller (*cyfarwydd*) was originally a seer and a teacher who guided the souls of his hearers through the world of 'mystery.'"

This is all the more true when the story is a mythological one, a sacred story. Mythology is a symbolic way of looking at the world. Its concern is not to simply describe physical reality (the world of the five senses), but to make contact with the ultimate source(s) or principle(s) underlying physical reality. Mythology uses storytelling to give form to the unseen, so that the human mind can expand and begin to know the unknowable. Myths, therefore, operate on a different plane from that of science, history, or even fiction. They use symbolic language to trigger our deepest levels of connection with existence. A culture's mythology is its pathway into the mysteries.

The ancient Celts seem to have been well aware of the power of myth, and gave the telling of sacred stories a recognized and prominent role. According to a 10th-century Irish manuscript, a poet was expected to know 250 primary stories and 100 secondary stories. These tales, as we mentioned in Chapter 2, were organized according to theme: Feasts, Voyages, Adventures, Courtships, Births, and so on. It seems that one of the main reasons for this form of categorization was that the stories traditionally were told at corresponding events in people's lives. Alwyn and Brinley Rees (*Celtic Heritage*, p. 210) summarize the situation beautifully:

> "...a wedding-night, the 'warming' of a new house, the eve of battle, the bringing out of ale, feasts, and the taking over of an inheritance were some of the occasions when tales were traditionally told.... [T]hey were also told before setting out on a voyage and before going to a court of law or to a hunt. Again, storytelling was a feature of the celebration of seasonal festivals, while it has been the custom at wakes for the dead, at christenings, and at weddings down to our own day.... [W]e would suggest that originally there were tales appropriate to each occasion."

It is clear from all this that one of the best ways for us to carry on Pagan Celtic spirituality as a living tradition is to incorporate storytelling (or story listening!) into our lives as much as possible.

We can tell you from our own experience that something marvelous happens when you start telling the stories of the deities aloud. As the words flow through you, you begin to understand them differently. Certain parts of the story take on new meaning or importance to you. Often you see connections that you did not notice before. And the same things can happen to people listening to storytelling. They may have read the myth a dozen times and think they know it thoroughly. But in the presence of the living story, it all becomes new. A particular episode or character seems to speak directly to them and what they are experiencing in life. Or suddenly they see a theme or symbol in the story that they never noticed before, but that supplies them with the spiritual sustenance they've been looking for, perhaps without even knowing it. And every person in a storyteller's audience may come away with a different experience, a different insight. Moreover, the next time the story is told and heard, it may reveal entirely different treasures.

Can anyone tell these sacred stories? Well, people who have a natural flair for the dramatic probably have an easier time bringing the characters and situations to life. Nevertheless, we believe just about everyone has the potential to become a storyteller, as long as you're willing to put the appropriate amount of energy and effort into developing the art. The first step is to read the stories, perhaps in multiple versions and retellings. Take the time to think about them, turning them over in your mind, thereby anchoring them in your heart. Do some research into the stories' background—the culture and history of their land of origin. Get to know the characters (if they are goddesses and gods) through devotionals or regular meditation. Walk with them in your daily life.

Read the stories aloud to yourself. Throw yourself into it and act out some of the characters' actions, if you like. Let emotion enter your voice. Gradually, the story will come to life in and through you. To finish the process, you must let go of the book. Recite the story from memory to yourself, perhaps silently at first, but eventually aloud. And then, when you feel ready, tell it to another person.

You might start with a child—yours, or perhaps a child you are babysitting. Children can be a wonderful audience for storytelling—and by telling the great stories to children, you are giving them a marvelous gift: entertainment without commercialism. But more than that, you are also helping to foster the wonders of the imagination in them and introducing them to the great stream of wisdom that has flowed through the rivers of story throughout the centuries. You only need to bear two things in mind when storytelling to children: age-appropriateness and attention span. As children become more accustomed to listening to storytelling, their attention span (at least for stories!) will lengthen, and they will happily sit through long tales. And as children grow older, they can handle more sophisticated and morally complex stories—which can help them to process their own unfolding experience of life.

If you are a shy person or if you don't have a group of people with whom to share storytelling, you may not feel inclined to go much further with this process. And that's all right. Even if all you ever do is read the stories aloud to yourself, you are actively engaging with them, turning them into more than words on paper. You are giving them voice. In this way you give the Ancient and Mighty Ones voice, too, and bring them from the past into the present, into your life, and into the world that longs for their wisdom.

Appendix A

Taking Your Journey Further

In this book we have offered a broad spectrum of Irish, Welsh, and Gaulish deities for you to explore within the context of your spirituality. Do keep in mind that scholars have identified hundreds of gods and goddesses venerated by the ancient Celts! In other words, think of this book as merely a starting point on your journey into Celtic spirituality. To take your journey further, here are a variety of books we recommend, both for their scholarly accuracy, as well as their ease of use and relevance to Neo-Pagan spirituality.

Retellings of Celtic Myth and Lore

For the easiest way to explore the riches of Celtic spirituality, begin with modern retellings of the old tales. An excellent first stop on this journey would be Proinsias MacCana's *Celtic Mythology* (London: Hamlyn Publishing Group, 1970), an illustrated survey of the most important deities of Gaul, Ireland, and Wales. Anne Ross's *Druids, Gods, and Heroes from Celtic Mythology* (New York: Schocken Books, 1986) contains very accessible retellings of mythological stories from Wales, Ireland, and the Isle of Man. Tom Peete Cross and C. H. Slover's magnificent *Ancient Irish Tales* (New York: Henry Holt and Company, 1936) includes a generous sampling of stories from every cycle in the Irish tradition. Lady Augusta Gregory, the great playwright and friend of William Butler Yeats, penned two elegant anthologies of Irish myths:

Gods and Fighting Men (Dublin: Colin Smythe, 1976) and *Cuchulain of Muirthemne* (Dublin: Colin Smythe, 1970). For a more contemporary retelling of some of the tales, try Eoin Neeson's *Deirdre and Other Great Stories from Celtic Mythology* (Edinburgh: Mainstream Publishing Company, 1997). To enjoy a popular novelization of the Mabinogi, see Evangeline Walton's *The Mabinogion Tetralogy* (Woodstock, N.Y.: The Overlook Press, 2002). Peter Berresford Ellis's *The Chronicles of the Celts: New Tellings of Their Myths and Legends* (New York: Carroll & Graf, 1999) includes not only Welsh and Irish material, but also folklore from Scotland, Cornwall, Brittany, and the Isle of Man.

Translations of Original Tales and Poems

After you've gotten to know the tradition through modern versions of the stories, deepen your connection with the deities by reading the myths, which are often available in English translation. The Irish Texts Society has translated a large number of ancient manuscripts into English; Neo-Pagans will be particularly interested in *Lebor Gabála Érenn* ("The Book of the Taking of Ireland"), volumes 1–5 (Dublin: Irish Texts Society, 1938–1956) and *Cath Maige Tuired: The Second Battle of Mag Tuired* (Dublin: Irish Texts Society, 1982). The greatest of Irish Epics, *Táin Bó Cuailnge* ("The Cattle Raid of Cooley") has been beautifully rendered into English as *The Tain*, translated by Thomas Kinsella (Philadelphia: University of Pennsylvania Press, 1985). For Welsh material, one hard-to-find but essential text is *Trioedd Ynys Prydein: The Welsh Triads*, translated and edited by Rachel Bromwich (Cardiff: University of Wales Press, 1978). For the Four Branches of the Mabinogi, probably the best source is Patrick K. Ford's *The Mabinogi and Other Medieval Welsh Tales* (Berkeley: University of California Press, 1977); see also his *Celtic Poets: Songs and Tales from Early Ireland and Wales* (Belmont, Mass.: Ford & Bailie, 1999).

Interpretations of the Tradition

We believe the single best way to immerse yourself in the magical world of Celtic Paganism is to read, or hear, or in any possible way learn, the stories and poems of old. But sooner or later, these sometimes strange and mysterious tales will leave you with many unanswered questions; for this reason alone, exploring the many academic and popular books that seek to explain ancient Celtic religion and spirituality seems a logical next step. Far and away, the book to begin with is Alwyn and Brinley Rees's *Celtic Heritage: Ancient Tradition in Ireland and Wales* (London: Thames & Hudson, 1961), as it looks at understanding Celtic myth in terms of Pagan cosmology and Indo-European spirituality. For a more general introduction to Celtic Paganism, see Dáithí Ó hÓgáin's *The Sacred Isle: Belief and Religion in Pre-Christian Ireland* (Rochester, N.Y.: Boydell & Brewer, 1999). A very fun and accessible book that traces the journey the Túatha Dé Danann took to becoming the fairies in Ireland is Patrick Logan's *The Old Gods: The Facts about Irish Fairies* (Belfast: Appletree Press, 1981). If you'd like to consider the psychological dimensions of Celtic myths, start with Peter O'Connor's *Beyond the Mist: What Irish Mythology Can Teach Us about Ourselves* (London: Victor Gallancz, 2000). Finally, here are two in-depth sources on the popular goddess Brigit: Séamas Ó Catháin's *The Festival of Brigit: Celtic Goddess and Holy Woman* (Dublin: DBA Publications, 1995) traces the earliest origins of the festival of Imbolc, while Alexei Kondratiev's lengthy essay "Brigit" in Judy Harrow's *Devoted to You* (New York: Citadel Press, 2003) provides a perceptive overview of how today's Neo-Pagans can integrate these ancient deities into our 21st-century spirituality.

One of our favorite authors is Miranda Green, a Celtic archaeologist who teaches at the University of Wales; among her many wonderful books (scholarly, but accessible to the serious layperson) are *Animals in Celtic Life and Myth* (London: Routledge, 1992), *Symbol and Image in Celtic Religious Art* (London: Routledge, 1989), *The Gods of the Celts* (Surrey: Bramley Books, 1986), and *Celtic Goddesses: Warriors, Virgins and Mothers* (New York: George Braziller, 1995). Each of these books combines detailed archaeological and literary information with reasoned interpretations to provide a balanced overview of how much we really do know about the spirituality of our Celtic Pagan ancestors.

Reference Titles

Finally, it's important to have one (or more!) quality reference titles available to provide quick definitions and descriptions of key deities, themes, locations, and other aspects of Celtic tradition. Our favorite reference books include Miranda J. Green's *Dictionary of Celtic Myth and Legend* (London: Thames & Hudson, 1992); James MacKillop's *Dictionary of Celtic Mythology* (Oxford: Oxford University Press, 1998); Dáithí Ó hÓgáin's *Myth, Legend and Romance: An Encyclopedia of the Irish Folk Tradition* (New York: Prentice Hall Press, 1991); Daragh Smyth's *A Guide to Irish*

Mythology (Dublin: Irish Academic Press, 1988); and Bernhard Maier's *Dictionary of Celtic Religion and Culture* (Rochester, N.Y.: Boydell & Brewer, 1997).

ଓ ஐ

Alas, as of this writing (summer 2004) many of these books are out of print. Thankfully, online used bookstores have made it easier than ever for the serious student to acquire rare and hard-to-find books. Try Abebooks (*www.abebooks.com*) or Alibris (*www.alibris.c*om) to look for out-of-print titles.

Celtic studies is a broad field, with a variety of scholars and writers who have varying levels of knowledge, credentials, or influence within the discipline. Many of the books listed here are controversial, or have been criticized for this or that weakness. However, we've included these books because we believe that, overall, each one is a worthy title for the Neo-Pagan student of ancient Celtic spirituality to read and study. But we must insist that you approach the study of Celtic mythology with an open yet discerning mind: Question everything you read and weigh the evidence of any one writer against the perspectives of other contributors to our common body of Celtic-related knowledge. The more you study and the more you interact with others interested in this topic (whether in your community or online through e-mail discussion lists and bulletin boards), the more balanced, thorough, and well-rounded your knowledge of the old gods—and how best to honor them today—will be. We wish you great joy and delight in your continued explorations!

Appendix B

Recommended Listening

Music has always been an important part of Celtic culture, and it remains a great way to connect with the Celtic traditions. If you are short of opportunities to hear live storytelling or Celtic music performances, CDs can give you a taste of that experience. And if you don't speak a Celtic language, listening to musicians from Celtic countries singing in Irish, Welsh, etc., will help you forge this vital link to the living cultures.

The recommendations that follow are chosen from among our personal favorites and are meant just to get you started on the musical leg of your Celtic journey. As you continue on this path, no doubt you'll make many discoveries of your own. Meanwhile, we apologize if a few of our selections are a bit difficult to find; we recommend them anyway because we believe that they are well worth the effort it might take to track them down.

To experience true bardic storytelling and poetry, with harp accompaniment, look for these CDs by Scottish musician-storyteller Robin Williamson: *Gems of Celtic Story,* vols. 1–3; *A Glint at the Kindling/Selected Writings*; and *Songs of Love and Parting/Five Bardic Mysteries*. Robin also has some excellent harp-only CDs, including *Legacy of the Scottish Harpers* and *Celtic Harp Airs and Dance Tunes*. Finally, a number of years ago Robin recorded *Music for the Mabinogi*, which he composed for a theater production in Wales. At the time of writing, this has not been reissued in CD format, but keep your eyes open in case it ever is.

For an imaginative retelling of the birth of Taliesin, try to find the CD *Mother* by Gilli Smyth. The artist was a member of an obscure 1970s art-rock band called Gong; her solo album is quite hard to find, although it has been released on CD in France. "Taliesin" is the only specifically Celtic track on the CD, but many of the other songs have a general Goddess-spirituality theme.

For Welsh harp music, look for CDs by Robin Huw Bowen; one of our favorites is *Old Hearth*. Siân James is another fine Welsh musician, who sings and plays harp; her CD *Pur* provides a lovely and intimate listening experience. Most of the songs are traditional, sung in Welsh (the liner notes describe what the lyrics are about); the last track, "Cyfri'r Geifr" ("Counting the Goats") is an example of a song used in the singing contests that were part of many Welsh holiday celebrations.

The Welsh band Carreg Lafar plays traditional Welsh music, singing primarily in Welsh, with what has been described as an energetic "Gypsy" flair. Their CD *Hyn* begins with one of the traditional Mari Lwyd songs. The title track of *Profiad* consists largely of a series of triads; this CD starts off with a Midwinter wren song.

For a rare treat, look for *Beneath the Twilight* by Emma Christian. Emma is a wonderful singer and harper from the Isle of Man. All of the music on this CD is traditional, and all sung in Manx. Included are a song to Mannanan and an invocation of Saint Bridget.

There are a number of fantastic Irish musicians around today. Two we particularly like, who blend traditional music with their original work, are Áine Minogue and Máire Breatnach. Áine is a singer and harper with a number of CDs that speak to Celtic spirituality, including *Between the Worlds*, *Circle of the Sun*, *Mysts of Time*, and *Celtic Meditation Music*. Máire is a great fiddler and singer. All of the tunes on her CD *Celtic Lovers* are named for various figures from Irish mythology. Also look for her *Voyage of Bran* and *Dreams and Visions in Irish Song—Aislingí Ceoil*.

Finally, we'd like to recommend a band made up of descendants of the Celtic diaspora, Emerald Rose. Aptly describing their music as Celtic-American folk rock, they mix traditional and original material. Either way, many of their songs relate directly to Celtic mythology and the goddesses and gods. Listen for these songs in particular: "Fire in the Head," "Castle of Arianrhod," "Gwydion's Song to Lleu," "Merry Mayfolk," "Dagger of the Moon," and "World's Wedding."

Appendix C

The Celtic Fire Festivals

F or many of the deities we have discussed in this book, we have noted their associations with the seasons and with various holidays. Most important among these special days are the four traditional Celtic holidays widely known as the Fire Festivals. These feasts all involved the use of fire—in the form of bonfires, candles, or the hearth fire—as an agent of purification and blessing. Each festival was closely linked to the events of the agricultural and pastoral year, and at the same time carried deeper spiritual meanings—in the Celtic tradition, the physical and spiritual realms continually interact.

The Fire Festivals are commonly referred to by their Irish names (which are generally the same in Scottish Gaelic and Manx, with slight spelling variations), so that's what we'll use in the headings below. The dates given include the night before because, for the ancient Celts, each new day started in darkness. Therefore, Samhain, for example, is actually observed from sundown on October 31 to sundown on November 1.

Samhain (November 1)

Samhain, "end of summer," marks the beginning of the Celtic year. The Welsh, Cornish, and Breton names for November 1 all mean "First Day of Winter": Calan Gaeaf (Welsh), Calan Gwaf (Cornish), Kala-Goañv (Breton). October 31, in Welsh, is Nos Calan Gaeaf, "The Eve of the First Day of Winter." In traditional Celtic culture, winter stretched from Samhain to Beltaine, and the nights during this period were typically devoted to fireside storytelling. Neighbors often gathered together to listen to a local or traveling storyteller. While they listened, they worked at their winter crafts, such as knitting; carding wool; and making baskets, nets, and rushlights.

As the boundary between summer and winter (and between one year and the next), Samhain was a time that marked the crossing of boundaries—specifically, those between the living and the dead, between this world and the Otherworld. In ancient Ireland it appears to have been the occasion for reaffirming the bond between king and land. On a more mundane level, flocks and herds had come back from their summer grazing grounds, and now were driven between two bonfires. The animals that could not be fed through the winter would be slaughtered, their meat to be preserved and their skins to be tanned. The ancient Celts honored this sacrifice, understanding how the animals' lives fed their own.

Imbolc (February 1 or 2)

Imbolc is usually interpreted to mean "in the belly;" another name sometimes given to this holiday is *Oímealg*, which is said to mean "ewe's milk." In modern Scotland and Ireland, the more common name for the day is Lá Fheile Bríde (in Manx, Laa'l Vreeshey), "The Day of Brigit's Feast." In Wales the feast is called Gwyl Fair Dechrau'r Gwanwyn ("The Feast of Mary at the Beginning of Spring"), Gwyl Fair y Canhwyllau ("The Feast of Mary of the Candles"), or simply Gwyl Fair ("The Feast of Mary"); sometimes, Gwyl Ffraid ("The Feast of Brigit"). Breton uses Gouel Varia ar Goulou, "The Feast of Mary of the Light."

This day marked the traditional beginning of the agricultural year. Ewes were starting to lactate, signaling that lambing was about to occur. In many areas, Imbolc was the occasion for blessing farm tools, and the first plowing took place shortly afterward. Imbolc seems to have been very much a festival of hearth, home, farm, and family. In areas where Gaelic was spoken, this holiday was particularly sacred to Brigit.

Beltaine (May 1)

Various spellings of this feast name are common, among them are Beltane, Beltene, Beltine, and Bealtaine. Whatever the spelling, the meaning is "goodly fire" or "bright fire." An alternative Irish name is Cétshamain, "the first of summer" or "the beginning of summer weather." The common Welsh, Cornish, and Breton names all mean "First Day of May": Calan Mai (Welsh), Calan Me (Cornish), and Kala-Mae (Breton). An alternative Welsh name, commonly found in medieval poetry, is Cyntefin, "The First of Summer." April 30, in modern Welsh, is Nos Calan Mai, "The Eve of the First Day of May."

Beltaine marks the beginning of summer (which is why the Summer Solstice is regarded as Midsummer in Celtic traditions). Flocks and herds were again driven between two fires, and then they could be taken to their summer grazing grounds. The ancient Celts also lit bonfires on hilltops; when the fires died down, it was common for people to leap them.

As at Samhain, the boundary between the worlds was especially permeable—this was manifested by the life force pouring into the land, turning everything green. In fact, boundaries of all kinds were much looser than normal. Beltaine, and indeed the entire month of May, was regarded as a time for love without restraint. Young men made bowers in the woods for their lovers, and folklore suggests that, in many areas, people were temporarily released from the bonds of marriage. (For this reason, May was a very unlucky month for a wedding. Brides also avoided wearing green, because that was the traditional color for May Day dresses.) From at least the 13th century in Wales, maypole dancing was also a much-loved and enduring custom. Dancing, singing, games, and sports were the favored leisure activities throughout the summer.

Lughnasad (August 1)

Once again, we find many variations in spelling for this holiday name: Lughnasadh, Lugnasad, Lughnasa, and Lúnasa among them. It means "The Games or Assembly of Lugh." There is excellent evidence that this holiday was observed all over the Celtic world, with a major celebration in ancient times in Gaul at Lugudunum, "The Fort of Lug" (modern Lyon). This festival, along with the name for the month in which it fell, was taken over by the emperor Augustus. The Anglo-Saxon invaders of Britain also adopted this holiday and gave it their own name, Lammas ("Loaf Mass"), by which it is still often known in Wales and Cornwall. The modern Welsh-language name for the day is Calan Awst, "The First Day of August."

Lughnasad marks the beginning of the harvest season. By this point, ancient people would have been out, or nearly out, of the grain they'd stored from the previous year. Now the first of this year's grain was just about ready to harvest—truly a cause for celebration. At the same time, there was a degree of uncertainty present, for a bout of bad weather could easily destroy the entire crop. For this reason, folk tradition in Ireland long preserved stories and ceremonies involving a god or hero fighting off the evil forces that could endanger the harvest. Among the folk customs traditionally related to Lughnasad are horse races and other contests of skill, as well as pilgrimages to mountaintops (which have survived to the present day in Ireland, although generally in Christianized form).

Chapter Notes

Chapter 10

1. This version of the tale is from *Trioedd Ynys Prydein*, Triad 53: "Three Harmful Blows of the Island of Britain: The first of them Matholwch the Irishman struck upon Branwen daughter of Llyr...."

Chapter 11

1. In *Taliesin: Shamanism and the Bardic Mysteries in Britain and Ireland*, John and Caitlín Matthews title this poem "Taliesin's Song of His Origins" and render the phrase in question as "the angry, terrible hag."

Chapter 12

1. Some authors have suggested that the second element of Arianrhod's name may not be *rhod*, "wheel," but *rawd*, "mound, hill, fortified place." Most modern scholars, however, have concluded that *rhod* is the correct interpretation. In modern Welsh, incidentally, *rhod* can mean "circle" or "orbit," as well as "wheel."

2. A field guide such as *The National Audubon Society Field Guide to the Night Sky* can be a real help with this.

Chapter 15

1. Medieval audiences would have appreciated the wordplay here, since Manawydan's name had a homonym, *manawyd*, which meant "awl"— a shoemaker's tool.

Chapter 19

1. The Celts have always enjoyed puns and other plays on words, so it is worth pointing out that there is an archaic Welsh word, *gwydio*, which means "to lust, sin, or harm." Medieval Welsh hearers or readers of the Fourth Branch would certainly have appreciated this as an alternate or simultaneous meaning for Gwydion's name.

Chapter 23

1. Test the essential oil on your skin before your devotional. Some people find various oils irritating to their skin, and you don't want to make this discovery when you're in the midst of a meditation! If you have asthma or allergies, you may also want to test out any incense you plan to use ahead of time.

Bibliography

Bromwich, Rachel. *Trioedd Ynys Prydein: The Welsh Triads*. 2nd ed. Cardiff: University of Wales Press, 1978.

Campbell, Joseph, with Bill Moyers. *The Power of Myth*. New York: Doubleday, 1988.

Carmichael, Alexander. *Carmina Gadelica*. Hudson, N.Y.: Lindisfarne Books, 1992.

Cross, Tom Peete, and C. H. Slover. *Ancient Irish Tales*. New York: Henry Holt and Company, 1936.

Cunliffe, Barry. *The Ancient Celts*. Oxford and New York: Oxford University Press, 1997.

Cunliffe, Barry W. *The Celtic World*. New York: McGraw-Hill, 1979.

Davidson, H. R. Ellis. *Myths and Symbols in Pagan Europe: Early Scandinavian and Celtic Religions*. Syracuse, N.Y.: Syracuse University Press, 1988.

Ellis, Peter Berresford. *A Dictionary of Irish Mythology*. London: Constable, 1987.

Ellis, Peter Berresford. *The Chronicles of the Celts: New Tellings of Their Myths and Legends*. New York: Carroll & Graf, 1999.

Evans, H. Meurig, and W. O. Thomas. *Y Geiriadur Mawr: The Complete Welsh-English, English-Welsh Dictionary*. Llandysul, Dyfed: Gomer, 1997.

Evans, J. Gwenogvryn, ed. *Llyfr Gwyn Rhydderch: Y Chwedlau a'r Rhamantau.* Cardiff: University of Wales Press, 1973.

Evans-Wentz, W. Y. *The Fairy-Faith in Celtic Countries* (Introduction by Carl McColman). Franklin Lakes, N.J.: New Page Books, 2004.

Ford, Patrick K. *Celtic Poets: Songs and Tales from Early Ireland and Wales.* Belmont, Mass.: Ford & Bailie, 1999.

Ford, Patrick K., trans. and ed. *The Mabinogi and Other Medieval Welsh Tales.* Berkeley: University of California Press, 1977.

Ford, Patrick K., ed. *Ystoria Taliesin.* Cardiff: University of Wales Press, 1992.

Gray, Elizabeth A., ed. *Cath Maige Tuired: The Second Battle of Mag Tuired.* Dublin: Irish Texts Society, 1982.

Green, Miranda. *Animals in Celtic Life and Myth.* London: Routledge, 1992.

Green, Miranda. *Celtic Art: Symbols & Imagery.* New York: Sterling, 1997.

Green, Miranda. *Celtic Goddesses: Warriors, Virgins and Mothers.* New York: George Braziller, 1995.

Green, Miranda J. *Dictionary of Celtic Myth and Legend.* London: Thames & Hudson, 1992.

Green, Miranda. *The Gods of the Celts.* Surrey: Bramley Books, 1986.

Green, Miranda. *Symbol and Image in Celtic Religious Art.* London: Routledge, 1989.

Gregory, Lady Augusta. *Cuchulain of Muirthemne.* Dublin: Colin Smythe, 1970.

Gregory, Lady Augusta. *Gods and Fighting Men.* Dublin: Colin Smythe, 1976.

Guest, Lady Charlotte. *The Mabinogion: A Facsimile Reproduction of the Complete 1877 Edition.* Chicago: Academy Press, 1978.

Harrow, Judy. *Devoted to You.* New York: Citadel Press, 2003.

Jones, Gwyn. *Welsh Legends and Folk-Tales.* London: Oxford University Press, 1955.

Jones, Gwyn, and Thomas Jones, trans. *The Mabinogion*. London: Dent, 1974.

Kinsella, Thomas, trans. *The Tain*. Philadelphia: University of Pennsylvania Press, 1985.

Logan, Patrick. *The Old Gods: The Facts about Irish Fairies*. Belfast: Appletree Press, 1981.

Mac Neill, Máire. *The Festival of Lughnasa*. 2 vols. Dublin: Comhairle Bhéaloideas Éireann, 1982.

Macalister, R. A. Stewart, ed. and trans. *Lebor Gabála Érenn (The Book of the Taking of Ireland)*. 5 vols. Dublin: Irish Texts Society, 1938–1956.

MacCana, Proinsias. *Celtic Mythology*. London: Hamlyn Publishing Group, 1970.

MacKillop, James. *Dictionary of Celtic Mythology*. Oxford: Oxford University Press, 1998.

Maier, Bernhard. *Dictionary of Celtic Religion and Culture*. Rochester, N.Y.: Boydell & Brewer, 1997.

Matthews, Caitlín. *Mabon and the Mysteries of Britain: An Exploration of the Mabinogion*. London and New York: Arkana, 1987.

Matthews, John, ed. *The Bardic Source Book: Inspirational Legacy and Teachings of the Ancient Celts*. London: Blandford, 1998.

Matthews, John, with additional material by Caitlín Matthews. *Taliesin: Shamanism and the Bardic Mysteries in Britain and Ireland*. London: Aquarian Press, 1991.

McColman, Carl. *The Complete Idiot's Guide to Celtic Wisdom*. New York: Alpha Books, 2003.

McNeill, F. Marian. *The Silver Bough: Scottish Folk-Lore and Folk Belief* (Vol. 1). Glasgow: William MacLellan, 1957.

McNeill, F. Marian. *The Silver Bough: A Calendar of Scottish National Festivals: Candlemas to Harvest Home* (Vol. 2). Glasgow: William MacLellan, 1959.

Minehan, Rita, CSB. *Rekindling the Flame: A Pilgrimage in the Footsteps of Brigid of Kildare*. Kildare: Solas Bhríde Community, 1999.

Monaghan, Patricia. *The Red-Haired Girl from the Bog: The Landscape of Celtic Myth and Spirit*. Novato, Calif.: New World Library, 2003.

Neeson, Eoin. *Deirdre and Other Great Stories from Celtic Mythology*. Edinburgh: Mainstream Publishing Company, 1997.

Ó Catháin, Séamas. *The Festival of Brigit: Celtic Goddess and Holy Woman*. Dublin: DBA Publications, 1995.

O'Connor, Peter. *Beyond the Mist: What Irish Mythology Can Teach Us about Ourselves*. London: Victor Gallancz, 2000.

Ó hÓgáin, Dáithí. *Myth, Legend and Romance: An Encyclopedia of the Irish Folk Tradition*. New York: Prentice Hall Press, 1991.

Ó hÓgáin, Dáithí. *The Sacred Isle: Belief and Religion in Pre-Christian Ireland*. Rochester, N.Y.: Boydell & Brewer, 1999.

Owen, Trefor M. *The Customs and Traditions of Wales*. Cardiff: University of Wales Press, 1991.

Parry-Jones, D. *Welsh Legends and Fairy Lore*. New York: Barnes and Noble, 1992.

Pennar, Meirion, trans. *Taliesin Poems*. Lampeter, Dyfed: Llanerch, 1988.

Rankin, David. *Celts and the Classical World*. London and New York: Routledge, 1987.

Rees, Alwyn, and Brinley Rees. *Celtic Heritage: Ancient Tradition in Ireland and Wales*. London: Thames & Hudson, 1961.

Ross, Anne. *Druids, Gods, and Heroes from Celtic Mythology*. New York: Schocken Books, 1986.

Ross, Anne. *Folklore of the Scottish Highlands*. Stroud, Gloucestershire: Tempus Publishing, 2000.

Ross, Anne. *Folklore of Wales*. Stroud, Gloucestershire: Tempus Publishing, 2001.

Ross, Anne. *Pagan Celtic Britain*. Chicago: Academy Chicago Publishers, 1996.

Sjoestedt, Marie-Louise. *Gods and Heroes of the Celts*. Translated by Myles Dillon. Berkeley, Calif.: Turtle Island Foundation, 1982.

Smyth, Daragh. *A Guide to Irish Mythology*. Dublin: Irish Academic Press, 1988.

Stewart, R. J., and Robin Williamson. *Celtic Bards, Celtic Druids.* London: Blandford, 1996.

Williamson, Robin. *The Wise and Foolish Tongue: Celtic Stories and Poems.* San Francisco: Chronicle Books, 1991.

Index

About
the Authors

CARL McCOLMAN is the author of numerous books, including *366 Celt, The Complete Idiot's Guide to Celtic Wisdom, Before You Cast a Spell* (winner of the Coalition of Visionary Resources award for Best Magic Book of 2004), *When Someone You Love is Wiccan*, and *The Well-Read Witch*. Other writings of his have appeared in print or online in such publications as *PanGaia, NewWitch, Aquarius, Atlanta Celtic Quarterly*, and *Beliefnet*. He is the founder and co-facilitator of Brigid's Well, a Celtic spiritual community based in Atlanta. Carl lives in Stone Mountain, Georgia, with his wife, stepdaughter, and four cats. You can visit him online at *www.carlmccolman.com*.

KATHRYN HINDS is the author of more than 20 nonfiction books for young people, including *The Celts of Northern Europe* and other titles on ancient and medieval cultures. Her poetry has appeared in *SageWoman, The Red Queen, Hole in the Stone, The Lyric*, and other publications. Kathryn did graduate work in comparative literature and medieval studies, and remains an enthusiastic amateur scholar. She has been studying and working with the mystery traditions preserved in Welsh mythology since the late 1980s. Kathryn lives in the north Georgia mountains with her husband, their son, three cats, and two dogs. You can visit her online at *www.kathrynhinds.com*.